PUERTO RICO

PUERTO RICO BY ROAD

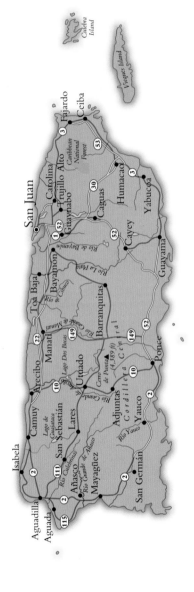

ATLANTIC OCEAN

Caribbean Sea

Culebra Island

Vieques Island

Mona Island

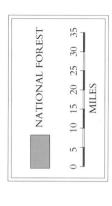

NATIONAL FOREST

0 5 10 15 20 25 30 35

MILES

CELEBRATE THE STATES
PUERTO RICO

BENCHMARK BOOKS

MARSHALL CAVENDISH
NEW YORK

Benchmark Books
Marshall Cavendish Corporation
99 White Plains Road
Tarrytown, New York 10591-9001

Library of Congress Cataloging-in-Publication Data

Schwabacher, Martin.
Puerto Rico / by Martin Schwabacher.
p.   cm. — (Celebrate the states)
Includes bibliographical references and index.
Summary: Describes the natural features, plant and animal life, history, government, and social life and
customs of the commonwealth of Puerto Rico.
ISBN 0-7614-1313-8
1. Puerto Rico—Juvenile literature. [1. Puerto Rico.] I. Title. II. Series.
F1958.3 .S39   2001   972.95—dc21   2001037674

Maps and graphics supplied by Oxford Cartographers, Oxford, England

Photo research by Ellen Barrett Dudley and Matthew J. Dudley

Cover photo: Tony Arruza
The photographs in this book are used by permission and through the courtesy of:
Corbis: 34, 43; Tony Arruza, 6-7, 27, 62 (right), 71, 84-85, 135; Dave G. Houser, 10-11, 99; Tom Bean, 13;
Kennan Ward, 16; Stephanie Maze, 18, 24, 79, 124; Kevin Schafer, 19, 20, 121 (bottom); Bettmann, 45, 47,
55, 87, 127, 128, 130; Wally McNamee, 48; AFP, 56, 59; Owen Franken, 61; Bob Krist, 68-69, 76, 83, 100;
Kit Kittle, 81; MacFadden Publishing, 93; Reuters NewMedia Inc., 94, 131; Macduff Everton, 112; Wolfgang
Kaehler, 120; W. Perry Conway, 121 (top); Mitchell Gerber, 129; Tony Roberts, 133; Jeremy Horner, 136.
Marine Images: Steve Simonsen, 15, 22, 66-67, 96-97, 109, 111. *Tony Arruza:* 25, 50-51, 62 (left), 77, 105,
107, back cover. *Photo Researchers, Inc.:* Larry Mulvehill, 21; George Haling, 63 (right); Jeff Greenberg/dMRp,
73; John S. Dunning, 117 (right); Gary Retherford, 117 (left). *Museo de Arte de Ponce, Luis A. Ferre' Foundation,
Inc. Ponce, Puerto Rico:* 28-29, 40-41. *The Granger Collection:* 32. *Instituto de Cultura de Puerto Rico:* 35, 41
(right). *Museo de San Juan/Municipio de San Juan:* 38. *Col. Museo de Historia, Antropologia y Arte, Universidad de
Puerto Rico:* 89. *Jack Agüeros and Curbstone Press:* 90. *Frank LLosa/frankly.com:* 114. *Luis Muñoz Marin
Foundation:* 132.

Printed in Italy

3   5   6   4   2

CONTENTS

PUERTO RICO IS . . .

Puerto Rico is a hot tropical island that is always in bloom.

"In Puerto Rico, you can't drive just to get there. You have to drive slow, and look at the trees, the flowers, the vegetation."
—innkeeper Roberto Prado

Its people are as warm as the climate.

"If you are Puerto Rican, *family* means anyone you've ever taken a bus with."
—teacher and poet Ana Betancourt

Life in the cities can be hard, but Puerto Ricans know how to get away from it all.

"If you want to get a driver's license, it will take you the whole day. But people learn to deal with it. On weekends, they go to the beach, or go to the mountains, and forget about all that."
—teacher Steven Greenia

Puerto Ricans have mixed feelings about being part of the United States.

"We stand as a nation surrounded by industry, but with little of it belonging to our people. . . . The United States controls our economy, our commerce . . . resulting in poverty for our people and wealth for the United States."
—nationalist leader Pedro Albizu Campos, 1937

"My parents saw the Americans come in. They knew what life was like before that. They were so grateful. There were no schools. It helped them."　　　　　　　　　　　　　—banker Marta Ramos

Their ancestors came from many places, but they are now one people—Puerto Ricans.
I am not african. Africa is in me, but I cannot return.
I am not taína. Taíno is in me, but there is no way back.
I am not european. Europe lives in me, but I have no home there.

I am new. History made me. My first language was Spanglish.
I was born at the crossroads
and I am whole.

　　　　　　　　　　　　　—poet Aurora Levins Morales

Puerto Rico is factories and palm trees, skyscrapers and remote mountain towns, universities and tropical rain forests. It is cars, coral, cliffs, and caves.

Puerto Rico has been dominated by outsiders for centuries, ruled first by Spain, then by the United States. Though many Puerto Ricans are proud to be U.S. citizens, some have not given up the dream of having an independent country.

Long before it was "discovered" by Christopher Columbus, Puerto Rico already had a name—the name used by the Taíno people who stood on shore to greet him. Five hundred years later, many Puerto Ricans still prefer to use this name. To them, their island is Borinquen, and they are Boricuas.

1 MOUNTAIN IN THE SEA

Puerto Rico is famous for its beautiful beaches, lush scenery, and warm climate. Located about a thousand miles off the southern tip of Florida, it is a true tropical island. It is part of a long chain of islands that stretches from Florida to South America, separating the Caribbean Sea from the Atlantic Ocean.

Puerto Rico is just 39 miles wide and 111 miles long. Yet on this small island live more than 3.8 million people, making it one of the most densely populated places on Earth.

A JAGGED LANDSCAPE

Puerto Rico is almost completely covered by mountains. The hills and mountains in Puerto Rico are not gentle, rounded curves. Instead, they have jutting points, like a cloth draped over a pile of furniture. They look like something out of a Dr. Seuss book.

A ridge of tall mountains called the Cordillera Central (cor-dee-YARE-a sen-TRAHL) stretches down the middle of the island from east to west. The Luquillo (loo-KEE-yo) Mountains guard the island's eastern tip. Some of the strangest mountains are in the northwest, in karst country. Karst is created when parts of the ground collapse, leaving odd, lumpy shapes. This happens when water flowing underground dissolves the limestone rock.

Flat, narrow strips of land run along the island's north and south

A view from the Ruta Panoramica, a scenic road that winds through the mountains of the Cordillera Central.

coasts. Puerto Rico's famous sandy beaches are in these areas, along with most of the island's big cities. On the island's eastern and western tips, the flat areas disappear entirely, as the hills go directly down into the sea.

LAND AND WATER

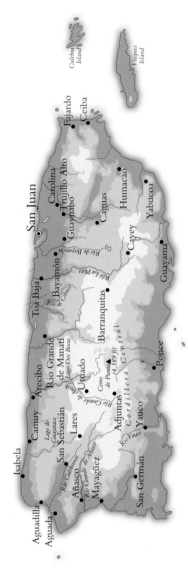

Offshore, Puerto Rico is rich in coral reefs—colorful, jagged structures built over thousands of years by tiny sea creatures. Coral reefs are a favorite haven for tropical fish, which makes them a great place for swimming, scuba diving, and snorkeling.

Some of the best places to see coral are the smaller offshore islands that are part of Puerto Rico. Seven miles to the east is Puerto Rico's largest offshore island, Vieques, where coral can be found right near the beach. A wilder, less populated island, Culebra, is

Some swimming spots in Puerto Rico offer more than just sand. This dazzling coral reef lies in the Vieques Passage, off Puerto Rico's eastern shore.

ENDANGERED LEATHERBACKS

Tired of always doing the same old things at the beach? On your next vacation, try something different—like rescuing a baby leatherback sea turtle.

The leatherback is the only turtle without a hard shell—instead, it has a leathery cover. Leatherbacks can grow more than six feet long and can weigh more than a thousand pounds. With their enormous flippers, they can swim thousands of miles through the open ocean, but they must come onto the beach to nest.

The Puerto Rican island of Culebra is a key nesting area for leatherbacks. Female leatherbacks crawl onshore, dig a hole, and lay their eggs. Seven weeks later, the babies hatch and scramble down the beach into the ocean.

The presence of people has made life difficult for leatherbacks. Electric lights confuse the baby turtles and cause them to crawl in the wrong direction. Construction and pollution destroy their nesting grounds. Some turtles are killed by boats. Others swallow plastic or get tangled in fishing nets and die.

In 1970, leatherback turtles were declared endangered. Now, each night from April through August, volunteers search the beaches of Culebra for turtle hatchlings. They guard the babies and make sure they find their way into the water. "It was super fun," recalled volunteer Lori Applebaum. "We had to go barefoot, because you don't want to accidentally step on them. We went out after dark with flashlights and pointed the way to the water so the baby turtles could find their way."

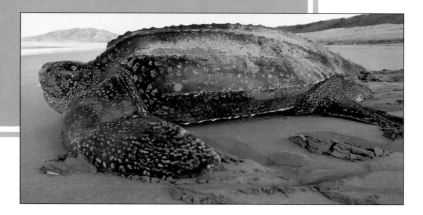

nearby. Parts of Culebra and twenty-three smaller islands are protected as the Culebra National Wildlife Reserve. They are home to large colonies of nesting birds, along with endangered leatherback and hawksbill turtles. To the west of the main island is Mona Island, which is surrounded by beautiful coral reefs. No one lives on Mona now, but it was once a hideout for pirates, and there are rumors that pirate treasure is still hidden somewhere in Mona's network of caves.

BIRDS, LIZARDS, AND SINGING FROGS

Puerto Rico is home to about 270 kinds of birds. Some, such as the Puerto Rican emerald hummingbird and the Adelaide's warbler, live only in Puerto Rico. Many of Puerto Rico's most common birds, such as the Puerto Rican bullfinch and the stripe-headed tanager, eat the island's abundant fruit. The Puerto Rican flycatcher, the Puerto Rican woodpecker, and many other birds feed on insects. The Puerto Rican lizard cuckoo hops from tree branch to tree branch snatching up lizards, while terns, coots, and herons feed in the water.

One of the island's rarest birds is the Puerto Rican parrot. Before Europeans arrived on the island, Puerto Rico was completely covered with trees. Back then about a million of these bright green birds nested in holes in tree trunks. Now most of the trees are gone, along with the parrots. In 1975, only thirteen remained. Today, breeding programs have raised their numbers to about a hundred.

For all the birds that live in Puerto Rico, there are even more lizards. In fact, for every seven birds, there are roughly 10,000 reptiles.

The Puerto Rican parrot lives only in Puerto Rico. It nearly went extinct when most of the trees it nested in were cut down.

Wherever you look, in the city or the country, you are likely to see a lizard. They come in many colors: brown, green, tan, speckled, or striped like a zebra. The largest of Puerto Rico's lizards is the rock iguana, which lives on Mona Island. It grows more than three feet long. The smallest, called sphaeros, can be as small as one and a half inches full-grown—including their tails. The lizards you are most likely to see are anoles, which come in many colors. If you look closely, they can be found sitting on leaves and tree trunks just about anywhere.

Puerto Rico's most beloved animal is a tiny frog called a coquí. Coquís are about an inch long, live in trees, and sing with a delightful pure, sweet tone. Puerto Rico has sixteen kinds of coquís. Some click, some warble, and some sound like an electronic toy. But the most common song is a two-note call that sounds just like its name: co-KEE, co-KEE. Each evening, coquí songs provide a cheerful tune throughout the island. "The coquí is very noisy, but it helps me sleep," says one boy.

There are almost no large mammals on Puerto Rico. This is not so surprising when you think of what it took for living things to get to the island. Seeds of plants and trees could be carried there by

Lizards are a common sight all over Puerto Rico.

birds, or float on the waves, or blow in the wind. Lizards could float to the island on logs. But there was no easy way for larger animals to travel from the mainland. The island's only large wild mammal, the mongoose, was brought by Europeans to catch rats on surgar-cane plantations.

Among the few mammals that made the long trip on their own were bats, because unlike other mammals, they have wings. Thirteen kinds of bats now live on Puerto Rico, ranging from small ones that eat insects and fruit to the greater bulldog bat, which has a two-foot wingspan and catches fish for dinner. Bats, like birds, help the environment by gobbling up insects and spreading the seeds of fruit trees around the forest.

Some places in Puerto Rico, such as El Yunque rain forest, contain 10,000 coquís per acre.

The flamboyan, or royal poinciana, has blossoms so bright it is nicknamed the flame tree. Brightly colored trees, flowers, and shrubs fill the forests and gardens of Puerto Rico.

BLAZING COLORS

Puerto Rico's real attraction for wilderness lovers is its dazzling plant life. Flowers that elsewhere would require careful nurturing in a greenhouse grow naturally in the hot, humid weather. Bright flowers such as orchids, bougainvillea, jasmine, and hibiscus grow everywhere.

A favorite tree is the flamboyan, or flame tree, which is lit up by

a blaze of orange-red blossoms that makes it look like it's on fire. Other interesting trees include the ausubo, which has wood so hard that it is virtually indestructible, and the ceiba, whose above-ground roots look like a tangle of octopus legs. In all, there are 547 species of trees native to Puerto Rico. Another 203 species have been brought there, including that symbol of island life, the coconut palm.

Though Puerto Rico's travel posters always show a beach of white sand, some parts of the shoreline are crowded instead with mangrove trees. These trees shelter much wildlife in their tangled roots. Oysters, lobsters, birds, and sometimes even blubbery, whalelike manatees feed there.

One of the most popular fish for anglers in Puerto Rico is the huge marlin. But other fish abound, from colorful aquarium-style tropical fish to hefty red snappers and tuna.

ENDLESS SUMMER

Nearly five million people travel to Puerto Rico each year to enjoy its endless summer. The average high temperature in San Juan is eighty degrees in January and eighty-four in July. It never snows in Puerto Rico—the coldest temperature ever recorded there is forty degrees. Though the mountains are usually cooler, the coastal cities can be hot and humid. On steamy days, says Basilio Graciani Peña,

The massive ceiba tree can live more than three hundred years. Its above-ground roots are so big that a person can stand nestled among them.

a San Juan cabdriver, "Even when it rains, you sweat." The air is so muggy, "It's like flan in your face." (Flan is a thick, sticky custard, a favorite Puerto Rican dessert.)

Just as the temperature hardly changes throughout the year in Puerto Rico, the seawater always stays around eighty-one degrees. But the slightly cooler temperature in winter is enough to keep Puerto Ricans out of the sea. "I would never go into the water in December. It's too cold," says Roberto Prado of Ponce. "But when tourists come down here from the States, they jump right in. For them it's like chicken broth."

Puerto Rico attracts millions of tourists seeking a place to relax in the sun.

Clouds gather along the ridge of mountains that form the Cordillera Central. It rains more in Puerto Rico's mountains than at the beaches, and it is cooler. Every five hundred feet higher you go, the temperature drops one degree.

CATCHING CLOUDS

Puerto Rico gets a steady stream of wind from the northeast called the trade winds, which sailors once used to travel the oceans. These winds bring clouds of warm, moist ocean air to the island. As the clouds reach Puerto Rico, they hit the Luquillo Mountains on Puerto Rico's eastern tip. As a result, it rains there almost every day, creating a lush tropical rain forest. This region has been preserved as the Caribbean National Forest, the only tropical rain forest in the U.S. park system.

All the mountains on the island receive a lot of rain. Since the land gets warmer than the ocean, the air over the island heats up. Hot air rises, so moist air is continually drawn up the mountainsides, creating towers of rain clouds. Clouds pile up over the mountains, erupting in thunderstorms even while it is sunny at the beach.

Since clouds usually approach the island from the northeast, there is a cloud "shadow" on the southwest of the island. On this side of the mountains, it is so dry that instead of lush green, you'll find a lot of cactuses and gnarly trees clinging to the bare rocks.

HURRICANE LANE

Though Puerto Rico is blessed with natural beauty and a pleasant climate, nature does present one major menace: hurricanes. Puerto Rico is directly in the path of the huge hurricanes that regularly sweep through the Caribbean. Their powerful winds can blow up to two hundred miles per hour.

Hurricane season lasts from June to November. During August the excitement and anxiety is at its peak. When a big one hits it can cause hundreds of millions of dollars of damage. After Hurricane Georges in 1998, "We went thirty-two days without power," said a resident of Bayamón. "My father didn't have any power or water for three months." Many people store water on their roofs and buy home generators for their refrigerators, just in case. But some things money can't replace. After Hurricane Hugo, in 1989, one

Puerto Rican recalled, "There were no leaves on the trees." People especially mourned the singing coquís that were washed away from their gardens.

Though people often lose water and power to hurricanes, few people worry about losing their homes. That's because most houses there are made of concrete. The thick boxlike structures can withstand just about anything.

Some of these houses don't even have glass in the windows. They just let the breezes blow through the shutters. When you live somewhere as beautiful as Puerto Rico, a cool breeze on a hot day is enough to make life look pretty good.

Powerful winds whip through the trees during Hurricane Georges, which left many people without water and electricity in 1998.

2 CENTURIES OF STRUGGLE

El Río Portugues y La Ceiba, by Francisco Oller y Cestero

Christopher Columbus was the first European to reach Puerto Rico. But he was not the first person to discover the island. Several groups of people had settled there long before Columbus arrived. For the people already living on Puerto Rico, Columbus's journey meant not a new beginning but the end of their way of life.

BEFORE COLUMBUS

The first people to reach Puerto Rico probably came by raft or canoe from the Yucatan Peninsula in Mexico. This peninsula juts out toward Cuba, the largest of a chain of islands called the Antilles that stretches from Florida to South America.

Around 2000 B.C., people from South America began working their way up the string of islands to Puerto Rico. They settled on the coast, where they lived by fishing and gathering food, and made tools from bone, shell, and stone. Another group from South America arrived between 400 B.C. and A.D. 100. They hunted with bows and arrows and slept in hammocks at night. They also made pottery and grew crops such as corn and sweet potatoes, which they had brought with them from South America.

The Taínos developed out of this group. They settled the entire island, not just the coast. The Taínos lived in villages of more than a thousand people led by chiefs called *caciques*, who could be either

THE CARIBBEAN ISLANDS

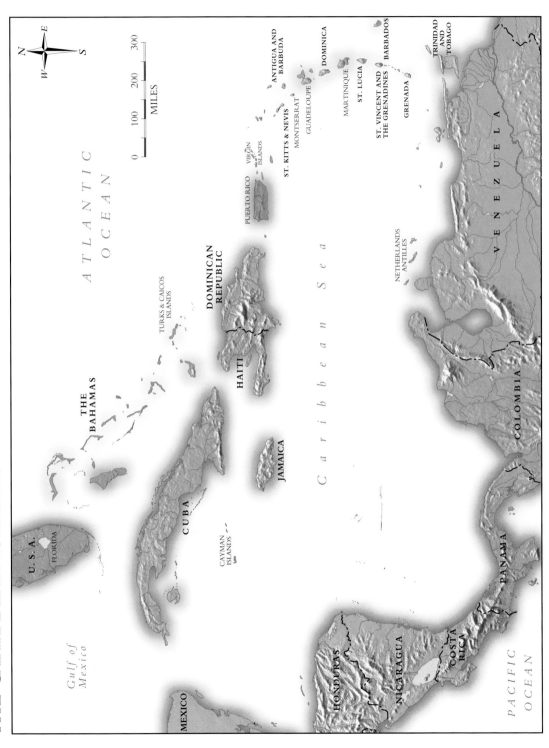

Christopher Columbus wrote of the Taínos' canoes, "A barge could not keep up with them in rowing because they go with incredible speed." The Taínos traveled by canoe to trade with other villages and other islands.

male or female. Large buildings made of wood with thatched roofs were shared by several families. Each village had at least one ball court, in which the people played a game that involved bouncing a rubber ball without using the hands or feet. Spanish observers said the courts were never empty. The Spaniards were astounded at how high the ball bounced, because they had never seen rubber before.

The Taínos were fairly small, the men usually just over five feet. They had high cheekbones, dark eyes, olive or copper skin, and perfect teeth. They traveled between the islands in canoes carved from a single log. Some canoes could hold eighty people. The Taínos were skilled farmers who grew foods such as cassava and sweet potatoes. The starchy roots of the cassava were ground and baked into bread. Corn, beans, and squash were all introduced to the Europeans by the Taínos.

THE FRIENDLIEST PEOPLE IN THE WORLD

A new wave of settlement in the Caribbean began in 1492 when Italian explorer Christopher Columbus sailed across the Atlantic in hopes of discovering a new route from Europe to Asia. Instead, he stumbled on the Americas. The news caused a sensation in Spain. The royal family, who had sponsored his trip, immediately sent him back. On November 19, 1493, he landed on Puerto Rico.

Columbus found a thriving island of 30,000 to 70,000 Taínos. He received a friendly welcome. Because the Taínos painted their bodies for important ceremonies, often using a red dye, these early meetings may have given birth to the idea that Native Americans have red skin, a myth that has never totally died out.

Columbus called the island San Juan Bautista ("St. John the Baptist" in Spanish). About fifteen years after Columbus's visit, a new representative of the Spanish crown named Juan Ponce de León arrived. He renamed the island Puerto Rico, which means "rich port." He also established the island's first Spanish settlement, Caparra, which was later moved and became known as San Juan.

Ponce de León's job was to turn the island into a colony—a place ruled and used by a foreign power. "There will be no problem, your

Columbus received a friendly welcome when he landed on the island of Borinquen, the Taíno name for Puerto Rico.

highness," he wrote back to the king. "These are the friendliest people in the world." Though fewer in numbers, the Spaniards had better weapons than the Taínos. They soon enslaved the Taínos and forced them to search for gold. Within fifteen years, most of the Taínos had died from starvation or disease. About the only Taínos left were those who had escaped into the mountains.

The Spaniards divided the island into large farms called plantations, where they grew sugarcane. In 1518, they began importing slaves from Africa to work in the fields. By the mid-1500s, however, the Puerto Rican sugar industry had fallen behind that of neighboring islands. For the next two hundred years, Puerto Rico was mostly used as a military outpost.

Over the years, San Juan suffered many attacks. In 1595, the Spaniards barely fought off the English pirate Sir Francis Drake. Three years later, when Spanish troops were weakened by illness, the English Earl of Cumberland captured San Juan. The same disease then struck the English. After six hundred British troops died in six weeks, Cumberland withdrew. Then, in 1625, Dutch invaders laid siege to San Juan and burned much of the city. But these were

An etching by Peter Schenck showing San Juan in 1625. Puerto Rico's major city is located at the island's best natural harbor.

EL AZUCARERO
(THE SUGARCANE WORKER)

Though harvesting sugarcane is backbreaking work, in this song the worker takes pride in the fruit of his labor.

Allí está el azucarero,
Cual abeja colosal,
Que en provecho de nosotros
Va formando su panal.

See! there stands the sugar worker,
Like a great and skillfull bee,
Forming, with his work, the beehive
That provides for you and me.

Chorus

merely brief interruptions in a period of Spanish rule that would last four centuries.

THE JÍBAROS

Even as the Spaniards used the best farmland along the coasts for plantations, independent farmers called *jíbaros* (HEE-ba-roce) survived on small farms in the mountains. Many were of mixed race,

A 1776 self-portrait by Luis Paret, dressed as a jíbaro. The hardworking jíbaros were known for their generosity, kindness, wit, and hope in the face of difficulties.

the children of Spanish immigrants, Taínos, and escaped African slaves. Their mountain farms were so remote and isolated that they had little direct contact with the Spanish authorities.

The popular image of the jíbaro is of a proud, self-reliant farmer, with a straw hat and a large knife called a machete. The jíbaro symbolizes freedom and independence to Puerto Ricans, much as the cowboy represents the spirit of the American West in the United States. Jíbaro traditions such as taking in travelers and helping neighbors through hard times live on in Puerto Rico today.

UNDER THE YOKE

Through the 1700s and 1800s, the Spaniards turned more and more land into large plantations. By law, anyone who did not own land had to work for a large landowner. This policy was designed to turn the independent jíbaros into plantation laborers. Unemployment was a crime punishable by jail or beatings.

Starting in 1849, all farm workers were required to carry a black book called a *libreta*. Anyone punished for disobedience received a black mark in his libreta. This often meant no one would hire him, which resulted in further punishment for being unemployed. These hated books also contained records of debts the workers could not repay, which kept them tied to their masters like slaves.

The landowners and business owners were also chafing under Spanish rule. They paid heavy taxes to the king and were barred from trading with any country besides Spain—a law they often ignored.

Eventually, a nationalist movement arose seeking independence from Spain. Its leader was Ramón Emeterio Betances, who had

studied medicine in France and returned to treat the island's poor. Betances denounced Spanish rule, writing, "We have been paying immense taxes and still have no roads, railways, telegraph systems and steamships. The rabble of Spain—soldiers and clerks—come to Puerto Rico and squeeze us dry, returning to their homeland with millions belonging to us. The government prohibits schools, newspapers and books."

Betances organized a rebellion against the Spanish forces. A government spy discovered the secret plan, and several nationalist leaders were arrested. But a revolt took place anyway. Rebels captured the town of Lares on September 23, 1868 and announced the

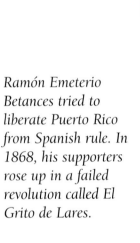

A painting of a Puerto Rican plantation titled Hacienda Aurora, *by Francisco Oller y Cestero*

Ramón Emeterio Betances tried to liberate Puerto Rico from Spanish rule. In 1868, his supporters rose up in a failed revolution called El Grito de Lares.

creation of the Republic of Puerto Rico. Though the rebellion was crushed, this day is still celebrated as a national holiday in Puerto Rico. It is known as El Grito de Lares—the shout of Lares—and symbolizes the Puerto Rican people's long-simmering desire to be independent.

In 1897, a change of power in Spain gave Puerto Ricans what they had long sought—the right to rule themselves. Puerto Rico was declared a self-governing state. It would have an elected congress that shared power with a governor from Spain. Puerto Rico's new government took control in July 1898, but it was short-lived.

The United States wanted to force Spain out of the Caribbean. As luck would have it, war broke out between the United States and Spain the very year Puerto Rico finally won self-rule. Less than a month into the new government, United States troops landed on Puerto Rico. They met little resistance from the Spanish army, and the war was soon over. After four centuries of Spanish domination, Puerto Ricans found themselves with a new colonial ruler.

AMERICAN RULE

"We have come . . . to promote your prosperity and bestow upon you the . . . blessing of the liberal institutions of our government," announced the conquering U.S. general, Nelson Miles. Preferring independence to such blessings, Betances angrily predicted that "If Puerto Rico does not act fast, it will be an American colony forever." Both were partly right. American rule brought many improvements, but a hundred years later, Puerto Rico still would not be independent.

When the United States took over, 80 percent of Puerto Ricans lived in thatched huts with no electricity. Only one out of ten children attended school. Health and education improved under the Americans. New roads and electric lines spanned the island, and many schools were built.

The United States created a Puerto Rican house of delegates, but it had little power. When Puerto Ricans became U.S. citizens in 1917, they were not even consulted. Still, 18,000 of these new

A hut in the mountains of the Caribbean National Forest made from palms, poles, and vines.

citizens served in the armed forces when the United States entered World War I that same year.

After World War I, American businesses, such as the Amalgamated Sugar Company, bought the best farmland in Puerto Rico.

While some jíbaros still lived in the mountains, most Puerto Ricans worked for foreigners under harsh conditions. One man who worked for Amalgamated Sugar remembered, "If we stopped work to rest a moment, they would come and spit on us and kick us, beat us with barber straps."

THE FIGHT FOR SELF-GOVERNMENT

In the 1930s, a new nationalist movement arose under a lawyer named Pedro Albizu Campos. He argued that because Puerto Rico was a free state when it was invaded by the United States, the two countries were still at war. During a nationalist rally at the University of Puerto Rico in 1935, several demonstrators were killed. Two nationalists retaliated by shooting the police chief. The killers were arrested and beaten to death, and Albizu Campos and seven other nationalist leaders were sent to prison. Protests continued, and during a peaceful demonstration in Ponce in 1937, Puerto Rican police killed nineteen nationalist demonstrators and wounded one hundred more in what is known as the Ponce Massacre.

Albizu Campos returned ten years later to find the movement still alive. In 1950, nationalists stormed the police station in San Juan, the town hall in Mayagüez, and the mayor's office in Lares. In 1950, two gunmen attacked the residence of U.S. president Harry Truman, and in 1954, nationalists entered the U.S. House of Representatives and shot five congressmen.

But no matter how passionate the nationalists were, they never received widespread backing from the Puerto Rican people. Most people had thrown their support behind a more moderate leader,

Luis Muñoz Marín. Early in his career, Muñoz Marín had said, "What finer goal could we have than our full independence?" But he came to believe that the way to improve Puerto Rico was to work with the United States, not against it.

Muñoz Marín started the Popular Democratic Party, known by its Spanish initials as the PPD. The PPD appealed to working people

After a nationalist rebellion in 1950, which included an attack on U.S. president Harry Truman and uprisings in several Puerto Rican cities, the Puerto Rican National Guard rounded up hundreds of suspected rebels.

with the slogan *Pan, Tierra, y Libertad* (Bread, Land, and Liberty) and offered them rent-free government land. In 1948, when Puerto Ricans were allowed for the first time to elect their governor themselves, they chose Muñoz Marín.

By this time, Muñoz Marín had backed away from the goal of independence in favor of a compromise. Puerto Rico would have its own government, but it would remain part of the United States as a commonwealth. Puerto Ricans voted for the new arrangement in 1951, and their new constitution went into effect in 1952.

OPERATION BOOTSTRAP

Muñoz Marín and the U.S. Congress came up with a plan to develop Puerto Rico's economy. Known as Operation Bootstrap, the plan called for U.S. companies to build factories on the island to employ Puerto Rican workers. In return, the businesses would pay no taxes for seventeen years.

From 1947 to 1960, the number of factories in Puerto Rico increased from one hundred to six hundred. By 1955, manufacturing was a bigger part of the island's economy than farming. Hospitals and schools were built, teachers and doctors were trained, and highways and houses were constructed.

Though U.S. president Dwight Eisenhower called it "the single most impressive plan of economic development in the free world," Operation Bootstrap could not come close to employing all of Puerto Rico's people. Thousands of people moved from the countryside to the cities in search of jobs that weren't there.

To ease unemployment, the Puerto Rican and U.S. governments

Puerto Rican women work on an assembly line making electronic products. Many American companies built factories in Puerto Rico as part of Operation Bootstrap.

urged people to move to the United States. As Muñoz Marín put it, "Our problem was there weren't enough jobs for the people and we couldn't bring the jobs in fast enough. Some people had to leave." Billboards urged people to move to New York, and the government

Rather than joining the U.S. Olympic team, Puerto Ricans send their own team to the Olympics. At the 1996 Olympics, the U.S. softball team played Puerto Rico.

helped pay their way. Large Puerto Rican communities sprang up in New York and other cities.

But even a massive migration that would bring more than 2 million Puerto Ricans to the mainland was not enough to erase the unemployment problem. One controversial method the government used to keep the population down was to give women operations that made it impossible for them to have more babies. Some women were asked to agree to the operation right after giving birth. Many did not understand that it was permanent. By 1965, a third of all women of childbearing age had been sterilized.

Pollution was another cost of Operation Bootstrap. Oil and chemical plants along the south coast have shortened lifespans in some areas by ten years. Pollution and overfishing ruined the fishing industry. In the 1960s, four thousand pounds of fish were caught in the Manatí River each year. The river became so polluted by American drug factories that by 1976, only forty pounds of fish were caught in the brown, smelly water. Despite a natural bounty that could once feed its people five times over, Puerto Rico now imports food from the mainland.

PASSIONATE DEBATE

The debate over whether to tighten or loosen the island's ties to the United States continues to dominate Puerto Rican politics. Puerto Rico is poorer than any of the fifty U.S. states. But Puerto Ricans are better off than their Caribbean neighbors, who do not have the right to work in the United States because they are not U.S. citizens. Though Puerto Ricans are proud and independent-minded, few want to face the uncertain economic future that would come with independence.

In 1968, a new party was formed to promote the idea that Puerto Rico should become the fifty-first U.S. state. Since then, the New Progressive Party has exchanged power with the PPD several times. A century after the arrival of U.S. troops, popular opinion over Puerto Rico's future remains as passionate and divided as ever.

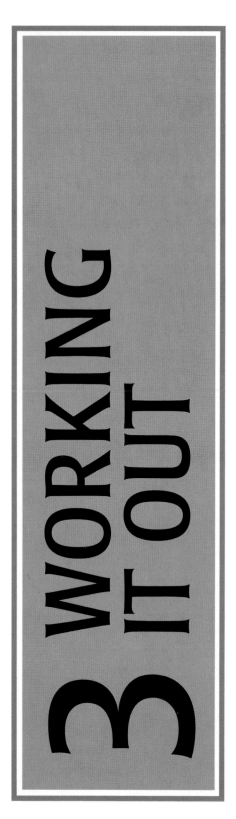

3 WORKING IT OUT

The capitol in San Juan

Puerto Rico is neither a state nor a country, but something in between—a commonwealth. It is considered an "associated free state" voluntarily linked to the United States, but it is not free to end this association unless the United States agrees.

Puerto Rico's government is similar to that of a U.S. state. Puerto Ricans elect a legislature that passes laws governing the island, but the U.S. government retains many important powers. The Puerto Rican government runs the schools, roads, and police, while U.S. laws regulate the environment, labor rules, and trade with other countries.

Puerto Ricans are U.S. citizens, but they do not vote in U.S. presidential elections or pay federal taxes, unless they move to a U.S. state. The U.S. government pays for many programs in Puerto Rico, but Puerto Ricans have no senators or representatives in the U.S. Congress, just one nonvoting delegate.

INSIDE GOVERNMENT

Like the United States, Puerto Rico has three branches of government, legislative, executive, and judicial.

Legislative. The legislative branch consists of a senate and house of representatives, whose members propose and vote on the laws of Puerto Rico. Senators and representatives are elected to

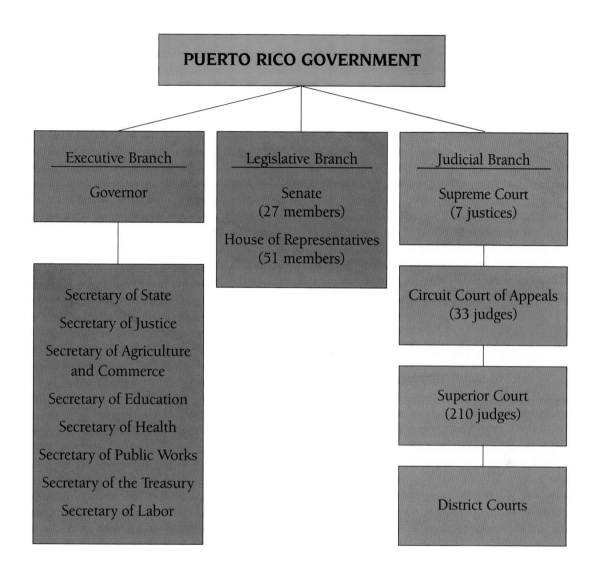

PUERTO RICO GOVERNMENT

Executive Branch

Governor

Secretary of State

Secretary of Justice

Secretary of Agriculture
and Commerce

Secretary of Education

Secretary of Health

Secretary of Public Works

Secretary of the Treasury

Secretary of Labor

Legislative Branch

Senate
(27 members)

House of Representatives
(51 members)

Judicial Branch

Supreme Court
(7 justices)

Circuit Court of Appeals
(33 judges)

Superior Court
(210 judges)

District Courts

four-year terms. The house of representatives includes one member from each of forty districts, plus eleven representatives-at-large, who represent the entire island instead of one district. The senate has two members from each of eight districts, plus eleven senators-at-large. If one party controls more than two-thirds of either house, however, more members are selected, until other parties have at least one-third of the total.

Executive. The head of the executive branch is the governor, who is elected to a four-year term. The governor appoints many important officials, including a council of secretaries who run various departments. The governor can veto bills passed by the legislature, which prevents them from becoming law. But if two-thirds of both the house and the senate vote for the bill again, it becomes a law. In 2000, Puerto Ricans elected their first female governor, Sila Calderón, a former mayor of San Juan.

Judicial. The judicial branch is headed by judges, who decide how to apply the law to settle disputes. Most trials of serious crimes are held in the superior court. If someone disagrees with a ruling in the superior court, they can ask the court of appeals to review the case. If appealed again, Puerto Rico's supreme court makes a final judgment. The supreme court's seven justices are appointed by the governor and approved by the senate. They serve until age seventy. The governor also appoints judges to the superior court and the circuit court of appeals.

THE STATUS QUESTION

The issue that has dominated political debate ever since the U.S. invasion in 1898 is what form of government Puerto Rico should have. Specifically, people argue about how closely Puerto Rico should be tied to the United States. Staying a commonwealth, writer Esmerelda Santiago contends, is a way to hide from "the

DOÑA FELA

One of Puerto Rico's most popular politicians, Felisa Rincón de Gautier, had a career that spanned the twentieth century. Born in Ceiba in 1897, she entered politics by helping Puerto Rican women win the right to vote in 1932. She then helped Luis Muñoz Marín create the PPD in 1938. Eight years later, she was elected mayor of San Juan, a job she held for twenty-two years. As mayor, she set up a system of direct contact with every neighborhood in San Juan, which kept her informed about the needs of the city's poorest citizens. She was also active in politics in the United States, where she helped launch the Head Start program that provides poor children with a preschool education.

Doña Fela, as she was popularly known, was beloved by many Puerto Ricans. She once sent an airplane full of snow to Puerto Rico, because the children had never seen snow before. Doña Fela died in 1994 at age ninety-seven.

Puerto Ricans have a strong sense of national identity, but they are divided over whether to remain a commonwealth, become a state, or become independent. According to writer Esmerelda Santiago, "In our hearts, we want to believe independence is the right choice, but our history forces us to see it as a lost cause."

question of who we are as a people . . . . It is not a choice. It is a refusal to choose."

Statehood would give Puerto Rico representation in the U.S. Congress. But it would also force individuals and businesses to pay U.S. taxes. "Statehood?" scoffs one resident. "The fat cats would never let it happen. They don't want the taxman down here." And many people worry that if Puerto Rico was absorbed into the United States, it might lose its unique culture.

Nationalists argue that ties to the United States harm Puerto Rico by making it dependent on outside aid. U.S. government spending provides Puerto Ricans with roads, schools, housing, food, and health care. More than half of Puerto Rico's residents receive food stamps. One North American who moved to Puerto Rico believes U.S. government handouts have eroded people's work ethic and self-respect. "It's our fault," he says. "We did it to them. You give a man food and a place to live without working, and you destroy him."

For many Puerto Ricans, the desire for independence is outweighed by the knowledge that most of their neighbors in the Caribbean are even poorer. They don't like being dependent on outsiders, but the alternative seems worse. Independence would mean losing U.S. citizenship, and with it the right to live and work in the United States.

"I personally doubt that Puerto Rico will ever be independent," says Marta Ramos, an officer at Puerto Rico's largest bank. "We're too Americanized, too used to American ways—cars, jobs, U.S. money. We're economically dependent. All the road money comes from the department of transportation. All the social programs, all the money comes from the U.S. To call all that off, and try to start on your own—it's not going to happen. We don't have the resources. We have beautiful beaches, but that's not going to support an economy."

So the debate continues. In recent years, a growing number of voters have supported closer ties to the mainland. In 1993, 49 percent of Puerto Rican voters supported commonwealth status, with 46 percent for statehood and 4 percent for independence. In 1998, 47 percent supported statehood, while 50 percent rejected statehood, the commonwealth, and independence. They voted instead for "none of the above," indicating that while many are frustrated with the present arrangement, they don't see an easy way to improve it.

FIGHTING OVER VIEQUES

An even hotter issue in recent years than Puerto Rico's constitutional status is the dispute with the U.S. Navy over the island of Vieques. During World War II, the U.S. Congress passed a law allowing the navy to seize Vieques for military purposes. In 1948, after the war was over, the navy used the law to take control of three-fourths of the island, which it has used ever since for bombing practice and mock invasions.

For years, Puerto Rican nationalists protested the military occupation of the island, which is home to nine thousand people. Then, in April 1999, a security guard was killed by a navy bomb that missed its target, and the movement gained much wider support. Large demonstrations became common, and hundreds of protesters were arrested.

Besides objecting to the explosions nearby, Vieques residents have also complained that metals such as lead and mercury in some bombs poison the environment. People on Vieques are 26 percent more likely to get cancer than those on Puerto Rico's main island. The navy insists the bombing on Vieques is not hazardous. But as one skeptic put it, "Why don't they use Nantucket or Staten Island, if it's so safe?"

The protests have attracted politicians from all political viewpoints, from those for independence to those who want Puerto Rico

On April 19, 2000, one year after a U.S. Navy bomb accidentally killed a security guard on Vieques, protestors gathered outside the White House in Washington, D.C., to demand an end to the bombing.

to become a state. Why would pro-statehood politicians take on the United States over Vieques? Besides the issue's popularity with Puerto Rican voters, Vieques offers the potential for huge profits. The small island contains some of the last unspoiled beaches in Puerto Rico. With the navy gone, developers could rush in and build hotels and expensive homes. Ironically, keeping people out is what has kept Vieques beautiful. As one visitor to Vieques explained, "We wanted to find a place that wasn't superdeveloped, where there isn't a casino and where music isn't piped into the street." Some people argue that if the navy does leave Vieques, its beaches should be made into parks for all Puerto Ricans to enjoy.

MAKING A LIVING

Making a living in Puerto Rico has always been difficult. In the 1990s, it got even harder, when the tax breaks U.S. businesses received for locating there were reduced. Most will be phased out entirely by 2006, making Puerto Rico less desirable to U.S. businesses. Without the tax breaks, Puerto Rico will lose jobs to other countries where wages are lower. Businesses can hire workers in the Dominican Republic, a neighboring Caribbean country, for about one-tenth what they pay Puerto Ricans.

Although Puerto Rico has a strong university system, many people with college degrees have to move to the mainland to get a good job. "The kids that go to the university—when they come out, they can't find a job," says working mother Delia Morales. "A lot of kids end up working in fast food places."

Agriculture, once the main industry on the island, now employs just 3 percent of the workforce. Coffee is the island's most valuable crop. Fruits such as bananas, mangoes, coconuts, and pineapples are also major crops. Farmers raise chickens, eggs, and beef, while fish and lobster are harvested from the sea.

Puerto Rico is the world's largest producer of rum, a liquor made from molasses, which comes from sugarcane. Sugarcane, once raised on vast plantations, is still grown on the island. But since Puerto Rico produces 6 million gallons of molasses a year, and the rum factories

The main campus of the University of Puerto Rico in Río Piedras, near San Juan, is a center of political activism as well as education. "Everything centers around the university," says journalist Alfredo López.

use 36 million gallons, they now import molasses from the Dominican Republic.

Manufacturing accounts for 20 percent of all jobs on the island. Chemical and drug factories are common; more than one hundred drug companies have plants in Puerto Rico.

Stone, sand, and gravel are mined on the island. Political battles

The hills of Puerto Rico are an ideal place to grow coffee. Puerto Rican coffee is considered among the best in the world.

Copper is one of Puerto Rico's most valuable resources.

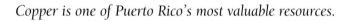

Though the fishing industry in Puerto Rico is not what it once was, fishermen still come up with some great catches, including these yellowfin tuna.

EARNING A LIVING

ATLANTIC OCEAN

Caribbean Sea

Mona Island

Culebra Island

Vieques Island

Aguadilla
Aguada
Isabela
Camuy
San Sebastián
Lares
Añasco
Mayagüez
San Germán
Adjuntas
Yauco
Ponce
Utuado
Arecibo
Manatí
Barranquitas
Toa Baja
Bayamón
San Juan
Carolina
Trujillo Alto
Guaynabo
Caguas
Humacao
Yabucoa
Cayey
Guayama
Guama
Fajardo
Ceiba

Lago de Guajataca
Río Culebrinas
Río Grande de Añasco
Río Yauco
Río Grande de Arecibo
Lago Dos Bocas
Río Grande de Manatí
Río de Cibuco
Río La Plata
Río de Bayamón

Agriculture

Bananas
Beef cattle
Coconuts
Coffee
Lobster
Milk
Pineapple
Poultry
Sugar
Tobacco
Tuna

Natural Resources

Lime
Salt
Sand and gravel

Manufacturing

Pharmaceuticals
Textiles

GROSS STATE PRODUCT: $41.1 BILLION
(2001 ESTIMATED)

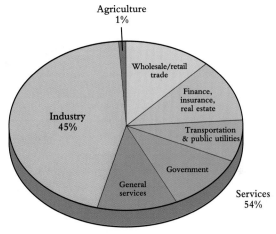

Agriculture 1%

Wholesale/retail trade

Finance, insurance, real estate

Transportation & public utilities

Government

Industry 45%

General services

Services 54%

also rage from time to time over whether mining companies should be allowed to dig up the valuable stores of copper and nickel in the central mountains, which would spoil their beauty. Puerto Rico's scenery contributes a great deal to the economy, as tourism brings more than $2 billion a year to the island and employs 60,000 people.

Much of the money earned in Puerto Rico, whether from manufacturing, tourism, or other businesses, eventually passes through the busy financial district in San Juan known as the Golden Mile, or Hato Rey. Skyscrapers there are filled with banks, insurance companies, real estate firms, and other businesses. The busy streets and business suits make Hato Rey look just like the downtown area of any other modern American city.

With the ocean on one side and San Juan Harbor on the other, the narrow strip of land called Condado holds many of Puerto Rico's largest hotels.

4 ISLAND LIFE

Puerto Ricans pride themselves on having their own cultural traditions that are separate from those of the United Sates. Their mixed feelings about being connected to the United States are shown in their views toward the island's official language. Spanish and English had both been official languages since 1902. But in 1991, the government made Spanish the only official language. Then in 1993, a new governor restored English to equal status with Spanish.

FRIENDS AND FAMILY

Speaking Spanish is just one of many cultural traditions that Puerto Ricans cherish. One they take special pride in is friendliness and hospitality to strangers. Someone you've just met for the first time will likely tell you, "If you ever come back, remember, you have another house."

Family is important to Puerto Ricans, who often have roots in the same community for several generations. Says one person with relatives in the small town of Yabucoa, "My mother has fourteen brothers and sisters, and except for one, everyone stayed in that town. You can imagine how many cousins I have." Though she moved to New York, she knows she always has a home to return to.

These family ties often go beyond close relatives. Years ago, children were often sent to live with relatives or close friends. Even

A Puerto Rican family in Yauco.

today, community ties are stronger in Puerto Rico than in the United States. According to a schoolteacher who moved to San Juan from the United States, "When you ask for help, you will have it."

COOKING WITH LOVE

If a friend introduces you to his relatives, expect to be asked to dinner. "Never say no if they offer you food," cautions one Puerto

ETHNIC PUERTO RICO

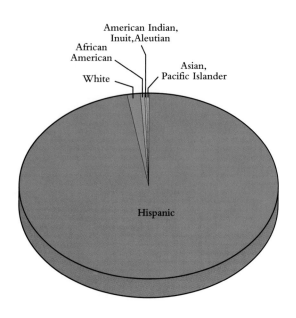

American Indian, Inuit, Aleutian

African American

White

Asian, Pacific Islander

Hispanic

Rican. Not only would it be considered rude to refuse, but you would miss a great meal. Simple foods like chicken just taste better there. "Puerto Rican chicken is the best in the world. Pork—you can't get pork like Puerto Rican pork. It's outrageous!" raves Roberto Prado, a hotel owner in Ponce who cooks for his guests himself. After eating his cooking, he claims, "You will wake up in the morning speaking Spanish."

Although much food in Puerto Rico is now imported, small farms and family plots still produce foods such as mangoes, avocados, and chickens. There are no chickens fresher than the ones people raise for themselves. In Puerto Rico, it is common to see chickens pecking away in a front yard, waiting to be fried up in oil and garlic.

Puerto Rican cooking should not be confused with Mexican food. You can find a dish called a *taco*, but in Puerto Rico, it is a soft piece of fried dough stuffed with seafood. Instead of spicy chile peppers, Puerto Ricans cook with savory seasoning mixes like *adobo* and *sofrito*. Meats are barbecued, as they have been for centuries—in fact, the word *barbecue* comes from the Taíno word *barbacoa*.

One of the most popular local foods is the plantain, which is like a giant banana. The yellow ones are sweet, and the green ones taste more like a potato. Plantains are cooked several ways. You can fry slices of green plantains in oil to make *tostones*. You can mash

The best fruits and vegetables in Puerto Rico are those freshly picked from nearby farms and sold at roadside stands.

BARBECUED CHICKEN WITH ADOBO

This recipe combines three Puerto Rican favorites: chicken, barbecue, and adobo. In this recipe, the adobo seasoning makes a tasty barbecue sauce. Have an adult help you with the cooking.

adobo

3 tablespoons vegetable oil
1 teaspoon chili powder
1/2 teaspoon garlic powder
1/2 teaspoon onion powder
1/2 teaspoon ground oregano
1 teaspoon salt
1/2 teaspoon black pepper
6 ounces tomato paste
juice of 1/2 lime

2–3 pounds small chicken parts
juice of 1/2 lime
2 tablespoons vegetable oil

Mix all the adobo ingredients thoroughly. Rub the chicken parts in juice from 1/2 lime. Spread vegetable oil lightly over the chicken.

Turn on the oven broiler. Place the chicken parts skin-side down in the broiler and cook for 12 minutes or until brown. Turn the chicken over and broil for 8 more minutes or until brown. Remove the chicken from the oven and spread adobo on both the top and bottom sides of the chicken. Put the chicken back into the broiler and cook until the adobo starts to char, about 5 minutes. You can also barbecue the chicken on a charcoal grill and use the adobo as barbecue sauce—delicious!

these fried pieces with garlic and pork rinds to make *mofongo*. Served with chicken or shrimp, mofongo makes one of the heartiest meals you'll ever eat. Another satisfying meal is the stew called *asopao*. But you can't go wrong eating chicken, rice, and beans in Puerto Rico. As one cook put it, "When you're cooking, the first thing you put in the pan is your heart. After that, it doesn't matter what you put in."

MUSIC AND CELEBRATION

Puerto Ricans enjoy many kinds of music, from classical to reggae to rap. The popular music styles heard most often on the radio are salsa and merengue, dance music filled with complex, fast-paced rythms. Delia Morales, a mother with grown children, keeps the radio tuned to a salsa station. "On Sunday, we usually go dancing. There are a lot of places with music on the beach," she says. "And you dance, you have a wonderful time."

Salsa means "sauce" in Spanish, and according to legendary drummer and bandleader Tito Puente, it is a mixture of "all our fast Latin music put together." Salsa emerged in New York, where Cuban musicians played with jazz musicians, mixing in rhythms brought to the Caribbean by enslaved Africans hundreds of years ago.

Other musical traditions go back even further. Instruments such as maracas, which make a rattling sound when shaken, were played by the Taínos. Stringed instruments like the cuatro were adapted from Spanish guitars and are still used today.

Any weekend is a time to socialize in Puerto Rico, but what really makes a Puerto Rican town come alive is a festival. Each year, every

Dancers in traditional costumes enjoy the evening air in Ponce.

town has a festival honoring its patron saint. They usually last more than a week, and by the final weekend, the town plaza is filled with music, dancing, and stalls selling tasty food. A wooden statue of the saint is paraded through town on the final Sunday. Each town has its own traditions relating to local history or legends. In San Juan, residents honor their patron saint, John the Baptist, by walking backward into the sea on the stroke of midnight, which is

AN AFRICAN FIESTA

In the seventeenth century, a fisherman in Loíza found a small wooden statue of a knight on horseback hidden in a cork tree. He took the statue home, but the statue turned up missing. He went back to the cork tree, and there it was. The fisherman took the statue home again, and once again it disappeared. He returned to the tree and found it back in its hiding place. This time, he took the statue to the local priest. The priest told him the statue was Santiago (St. James) and blessed it, which apparently was enough to keep the statue from popping back into its tree. Ever since then, Loíza has held a saint's day festival in honor of Santiago.

This festival is different from other celebrations, however, because Loíza, a town near San Juan, is composed almost entirely of people of African descent. Forbidden from worshiping their own gods by the Spaniards, the Africans used the saint's day festival as an excuse to celebrate their god Shango. Even today, an African influence can be seen in some of the costumes worn by the revelers. Traditional costumes include coconut-headed devils called *vejiantes*, tattered old men called *viejos*, and Spanish knights called *caballeros*. The elaborate costumes have made Loíza's festival the most famous on the island.

supposed to bring good luck for the coming year. In some cities, like Ponce and Loíza, the fiestas become carnivals filled with elaborate costumes.

The longest celebration comes at Christmastime, which in Puerto Rico lasts three weeks. Before the last day on January 6, Three Kings Day, children put boxes of grass under their beds for the kings' camels to eat. The next day the grass is gone, and the boxes are filled with presents.

MYTHS AND STEREOTYPES

Because of the flow of people back and forth between the island and the States, Puerto Ricans are very familiar with American culture. But many North Americans know little about Puerto Rico. Some assume that every Puerto Rican they meet is a criminal, because they have only seen Puerto Ricans portrayed as gang members on television. One Puerto Rican recalled, "In New Jersey, when I met the woman who became my mother-in-law, she thought I carried switchblades!"

"When you live in the States, you have to be perfect sometimes," says Jaime Morales, a young man who has lived in both the United States and Puerto Rico. "Some look at the person, but many think that because they reside in the U.S., they are somehow superior."

Most amazing to Puerto Rican businesspeople is the lack of basic knowledge they find among people in the United States, even those who work for companies that do business in Puerto Rico. "I encounter a lot of people who have no clue about where it is, what language we speak," said a Puerto Rican banker. She found that

Schoolchildren at play in Esperanza.

many North American businesspeople did not know that Puerto Ricans use American money. "There have been many instances when banks in the U.S. don't want to take our check," she says. Once she tried to subscribe to a major U.S. newspaper. "They sent back the check because they said they only took U.S. dollars—a newspaper!" she marveled.

If young Puerto Rican men face the prejudice that they are all in gangs, young Puerto Rican women face the stereotype that they are fiery or sexy. Writer Judith Ortiz Cofer believes this is due in part to "mixed cultural signals," because the clothing she grew up with on the island was more colorful and revealing than in the States.

Other assumptions about Hispanic people affect Puerto Ricans too. Once, just before Ortiz was about to give a poetry reading, "An older woman motioned me to her table. Thinking (foolish me) that she wanted me to autograph a copy of my brand new slender volume of verse, I went over. She ordered a cup of coffee from me, assuming that I was the waitress."

"I know that it wasn't an intentional act of cruelty," Ortiz continued, "yet of all the good things that happened that day, I remember that scene most clearly, because it reminded me of what I had to overcome before anyone would take me seriously."

A DIFFERENT TEMPO

Some stereotypes of island life, however, have some truth in them. The image of Puerto Rico as a tropical island with warm weather year-round is absolutely true. And with the easy climate does come a more relaxed way of life. Though this jam-packed island is no

With 3.8 million people on an island barely a hundred miles long, traffic jams are a common problem.

longer a wild, tropical paradise, some places still have a sleepy feel. "You're in the tropics now," one Puerto Rican explained, "and you have to learn to slow down. Take some time to enjoy the scenery."

"Coming from the States, it takes some time to adjust," says one frequent traveler. "Over there, everything is produce, produce, produce. Here you have to slow down. It's a different tempo."

Of course, there is a big difference between the San Juan area and traditional life in the country, or *campo*. One woman who lives just outside San Juan says, "If I go to New York, it's *too* crowded.

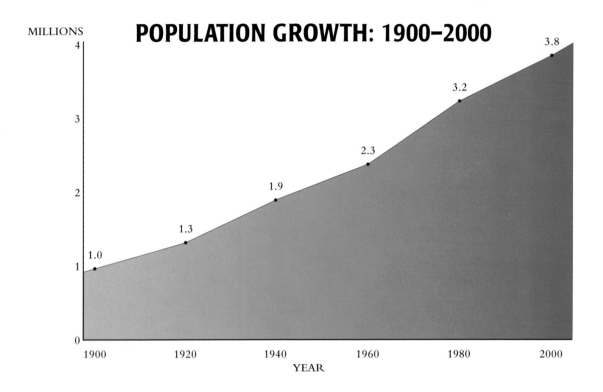

POPULATION GROWTH: 1900–2000

MILLIONS

1.0

1.3

1.9

2.3

3.2

3.8

1900 1920 1940 1960 1980 2000

YEAR

There's too much noise. Here it's calm." But when she visits her relatives in the campo, it's too quiet. "I can't go for too long to a place that's so quiet. I like to see people, hear noises, see people arguing. At my mother's, all you see is some chickens around, and some pigs. A week is good, but to live there, I wouldn't like it."

The stereotype of peaceful island life is certainly not true of Puerto Rico's crowded streets, where driving can be anything but relaxing. Waiting for a gap in the traffic is hopeless; you just have to plunge in. Longtime resident Susie Fairbank jokes, "Everyone drives really well, because everyone is such a bad driver, you have to drive really well not to get hit." Baseball star Sandy Alomar Jr. put it more bluntly: "Driving in Puerto Rico is crazy. If you don't drive crazy, they kill you."

Many city dwellers escape the madness by fleeing town on the weekends. No matter where you live in Puerto Rico, you are never far from a beach. "When you are there you feel free to do whatever you want," says sixth-grader Aura Alonso. "You always hear the music of the water." Sixth-grader Litza Acosta says, "I like to find shells and see starfishes. But the thing that I love the most is having time with my family at the beach."

"The thing that I like most about Puerto Rico is the beaches," says sixth-grader Sheila Roblejo.

5 THE PRIDE OF PUERTO RICO

Puerto Rico is home to a wealth of writers, artists, athletes, scientists, and political activists, all passionately committed to their work. Whatever their chosen careers, many of the island's most talented achievers display a concern for others that makes their fellow Puerto Ricans doubly proud.

PLAYING FROM THE HEART

The most popular sport in Puerto Rico is baseball, and the island has produced more than its share of major league stars. Recent greats include Bernie Williams, Juan Gonzalez, Ivan Rodriguez, and the Alomar family—Sandy Alomar Sr. and his sons, Roberto and Sandy Jr.

But Puerto Rico's greatest baseball star was Roberto Clemente. "Clemente is a great hero for all Latin players, especially Puerto Ricans," says Juan Gonzalez of the Texas Rangers. "Not only was he one of the best baseball players ever, but he was a great human being as well."

Roberto Clemente was born in Carolina in 1934. He joined the Pittsburgh Pirates in 1955. The following year, he batted .311, the first of thirteen straight years in which he batted over .300. Clemente was also a great fielder, known for running down fly balls in right field and rifling out baserunners at home plate. He earned

Roberto Clemente once said, "Anytime you have an opportunity to make things better and you don't, then you are wasting your time on this Earth."

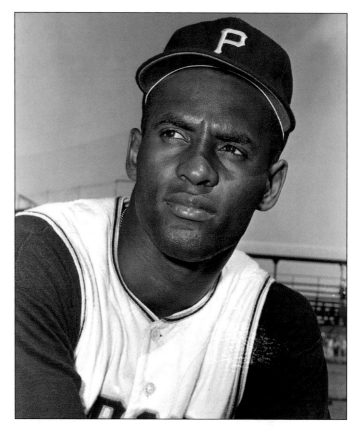

twelve Gold Glove awards for his fielding, along with four batting titles, and led the Pirates to two World Series championships.

But Clemente was admired above all for his character. In 1972, a terrible earthquake struck the Central American nation of Nicaragua. Clemente helped organize a relief mission from Puerto Rico. When the first shipment of clothing, food, and medical supplies was stolen, a second airplane was loaded with supplies. This time, Clemente got on the plane to personally make sure the donations reached needy Nicaraguans. On New Year's Eve, 1972, the plane crashed into the Caribbean Sea. Clemente and four others were killed. Clemente was immediately voted into the Baseball Hall of Fame, the first Latino to achieve that honor. Today, the Roberto

Clemente Award is given each year to the player who best represents Clemente's sportsmanship and community involvement.

PROTECTING HIS HOMELAND

Dr. Neftalí García Martínez is a hero in Puerto Rico for his tireless efforts to protect the environment. Time and again, he has used both vocal leadership and hard science to combat plans that would poison Puerto Rico's land, water, or air.

García, who was born in Trujillo Alto in 1943, has a Ph.D. in organic chemistry from Ohio State University. He has taught chemistry, environmental science, and the economic history of Puerto Rico at several universities. But his main goal is to use his knowledge for the public good.

García has long worked to educate and organize communities to protect themselves from dangerous pollutants. He often conducts scientific studies to provide evidence in conflicts between communities and industry. No issue is too large or too small. When a company wanted to build a landfill near Salinas, residents objected. They feared the garbage would leak into their water supply and pollute a nearby wildlife refuge. When the company claimed the landfill could not leak, García used his expertise as a chemist to show that even butter could pass through the dump's liner. When the U.S. Navy claimed their bombing was not harming Vieques, he wrote a study that concluded that the bombing "produced serious destruction of the mangroves, lagoons, beaches, coconut groves and other natural resources" and documented the island's high cancer rate.

García has written dozens of articles about environmental problems and ways to improve the economy without harming the environment. He has twice run for the Puerto Rican senate, raising public awareness of environmental issues. Without him, Puerto Rico would be a far less healthy place to live.

REVOLUTIONARY ARTISTS

Francisco Oller y Cestero, one of Puerto Rico's greatest painters, was the only Latin American member of the impressionist movement. Impressionism revolutionized art in the nineteenth century

A self-portrait by Francisco Oller y Cestero, one of Puerto Rico's greatest painters.

by using bold colors and loose brushstrokes to capture effects of light in nature.

Born in 1833 in Bayamón, Oller began his career studying the style of an earlier Puerto Rican master, José Campeche. He later moved to France, where he became friends with the great impressionist painters Camille Pissarro and Paul Cezanne. Oller then lived for a time in Spain, introducing that country to impressionism.

He eventually moved back to Puerto Rico, where he used a style called realism to examine social injustices such as slavery, which was not outlawed in Puerto Rico until 1878. In 1893, his most famous painting, *The Wake*, stirred up controversy with its critical portrayal of Puerto Rican society. Oller died in Cataño in 1917.

Poet Julia de Burgos also used her art to point out injustice. The

Julia de Burgos's very name is a statement of independence. She was born Julia Burgos Garcia. When she married her name became Julia Burgos de Rodríguez. Traditionally, "de" meant she "belonged" to her husband, whose name was Rodríguez. After she divorced in 1937—a daring act at the time—she took the name Julia de Burgos, indicating she belonged to no one but herself.

PRIDE AND PAIN

In these excerpts from Julia de Burgos's poem "Ay Ay Ay for the Kinky Black Woman," translated by Roberto Santiago, the author shows pride and strength in the face of injustice.

> Ay ay ay, I'm kinky-haired and pure black;
> proud my hair is kinky, proud of my fierce lips
> and flat Mozambican nose
>
> . . .
>
> They say my grandfather was a slave
> for whom his owner paid thirty coins.
> Ay ay ay, that my grandfather was the slave
> is my anguish, my immense sorrow.
> If he'd been the slave owner,
> it would be my shame.
> For with people, the same as nations,
> if being a slave means you have no rights,
> being a slave owner means you have no conscience.
>
> Ay ay ay, that the white king's sins
> be washed away by the black queen's tears.

oldest of thirteen children, Burgos grew up in poverty outside of San Juan, but with the help of local townspeople she was able to attend school. She graduated from the University of Puerto Rico in 1933, became a teacher and journalist, and published several books of award-winning poetry.

Burgos's poems are passionate and politically charged. They

probe the influence of racism, sexism, and colonialism on her personal feelings of pain and love.

Julia de Burgos died in poverty in New York in 1953, but a group of leading Puerto Rican writers and politicians had her reburied in Puerto Rico. Her fame has grown since her death, and she is now considered the greatest Puerto Rican poet of the twentieth century.

ACTING UP

For more than sixty years, Rita Moreno has been showing off her skills as an actor, singer, and dancer. She is one of the few people to win an Oscar, an Emmy, a Tony, and a Grammy—the entertainment industry's four major awards for film acting, television, theater, and recordings. Moreno was born in 1931 to a family of jíbaros in the Luquillo Mountains. During the Great Depression, her mother moved to New York. Though her father and brother stayed behind, Moreno began a new life in New York at age five.

By seven, she was already performing as a dancer in nightclubs, and at fourteen, she was working in films. Though she wanted to do serious theater, most of the acting roles available were as the stereotypical fiery Latina, "dancing barefoot and looking terrifically sulky and sultry," as Moreno once put it. She performed in more than twenty films in the 1950s before bursting into stardom as the strong-willed Anita in *West Side Story*. The musical won ten Academy Awards in 1962, including Best Supporting Actress for Moreno.

Her new fame led her to star in plays on Broadway. She has also appeared on the children's shows *Sesame Street* and *The Electric Company*, which gave her the chance to be a role model for Hispanic

Rita Moreno lit up the movie screen with her energy.

families. "I am Latin and know what it is to feel alone and ignored because you are different," she said. "My presence can tell a lot of children and some adults, 'Yes, we do exist, we have value.'"

When Benicio del Toro won an Academy Award in 2001 for his performance in *Traffic*, he established himself as one of the hottest young movie stars around. Unlike Moreno, who was often stuck with small, stereotypical roles, del Toro has been able to immerse himself in the more complex characters now available to Latinos.

Benicio del Toro accepts the 2001 Academy Award for Best Supporting Actor. "More than any other actor I've ever met, Benicio is not in pursuit of fame or recognition," says director Christopher McQuarrie. "He would rather create a character."

Born in San Germán in 1967, del Toro attended college in California before moving to New York to study acting. His work in theater drew the attention of film directors, who cast him in films such as *The Usual Suspects* and *Basquiat*. Del Toro sometimes goes to great lengths to adapt to his roles. For the film *Fear and Loathing in Las Vegas*, he gained forty-five pounds. "He's obsessed with his work," says the film's director, Terry Gilliam. "He draws the camera like a magnet because he keeps coming up with things that are dark, brooding, dangerous, and sexy."

What especially impresses people about del Toro is his intelligence. "Benicio has a wonderful mind," says his fellow actor Ed Harris. "It's a little like firecrackers going off; he's got these great ideas that just explode."

EL REY

Known as El Rey, or "the King," Tito Puente recorded more than one hundred albums and wrote more than four hundred songs. He performed in movies, on television, and at the White House, where President Jimmy Carter called him "the Goodwill Ambassador of Latin American Music." In a career that lasted sixty years, he never left his audiences disappointed.

Though Puente's parents were from Puerto Rico, he grew up in a Hispanic neighborhood in New York City. Puente began studying drums and percussion around the age of ten. "I was always banging on boxes, on the window sill," he recalls. He began performing professionally in his early teens, and at age eighteen his playing was so exciting that the band moved his drum set to the front of the stage, where he performed standing up to take advantage of his electrifying stage presence.

Puente attended the Juilliard School of Music, where he studied composition, orchestration, and conducting. His knowledge of music allowed him to meld different styles of jazz and Latin music, and he played a key role in developing the popular dance music known as salsa. In 1979, he started a scholarship fund at Juilliard for Latin percussionists, which he said "gives a young Latin percussionist an incentive to learn how to read music. . . . It's not only what you learn in the streets—you've really got to go and study." Puente died in 2000 at age seventy-seven.

6 A TROPICAL TOUR

Tourists who go to Puerto Rico and spend their whole vacation on the beach in front of their hotel are missing the point. To see what's special about Puerto Rico, you've got to get out and about. Puerto Rico is a small island, so you're never more than a day's drive from anything.

SAN JUAN

Fortunately for even the laziest visitor, some of the island's most incredible sights don't require leaving San Juan. A favorite spot is El Morro, the huge stone fort on a point of land protecting San Juan Harbor. Exhibits there describe the fort's long history of clashes with pirates, and Dutch, English, and American invaders. Rarely does history come alive in such a concrete way. El Morro's tower, still standing, was built in 1539. Shell fragments fired by U.S. troops during their invasion in 1898 are still stuck in the wall. The fort is also just a great place to explore. Its many levels and circular and triangular staircases make it feel like a giant maze.

An old stone wall follows the coastline to another fort, San Cristobal, which protected the city from land invasions. Behind the huge wall between these forts is historic Old San Juan. The neighborhood is filled with churches and museums that showcase the city's history, music, and art. But the main attraction is Old San

A view from El Morro, the fort that has guarded San Juan Harbor for hundreds of years.

Juan itself. A stroll down almost any narrow street reveals beautiful old houses painted pale lavender, pink, green, orange, or brown. Metal bars called *rejas* (RAY-hahs) crisscross the windows with lovely patterns, serving more as art than protection. Though there are

LA ROGATIVA

In 1797, Great Britain sent sixty ships and nine thousand men to try to capture Puerto Rico from Spain. English troops surrounded San Juan for two weeks. The people of San Juan grew sick and hungry as they waited for Spanish soldiers to rescue them.

According to legend, the English siege failed when Puerto Rican women made an appeal called a *rogativa* to Saints Ursula and Catherine. At the darkest moment of the seige, the Spanish governor called for all the women of San Juan to march through the town. The women carried torches, and the streets rang with bells. Hearing the noise and seeing the march by torchlight, the English soldiers thought Spanish troops had arrived, so they ran away.

Today, a statue called *La Rogativa* stands on a hill overlooking San Juan Harbor. The dramatic statue shows the women of San Juan marching through the streets to save their city.

PLACES TO SEE

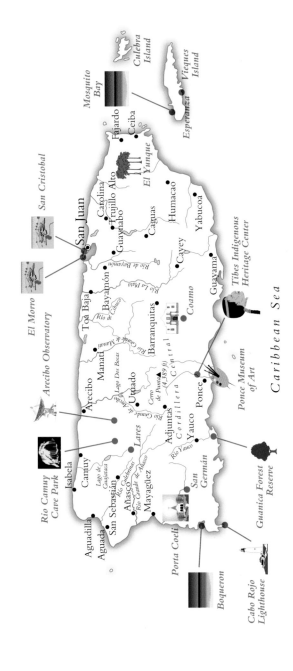

ATLANTIC OCEAN

Mona Island

Mosquito Bay

Culebra Island

Vieques Island

Esperanza

Fajardo

Ceiba

San Cristóbal

San Juan

El Yunque

Carolina

Trujillo Alto

Humacao

Yabucoa

Guaynabo

Caguas

Cayey

El Morro

Toa Baja

Bayamón

Río de Bayamón

Río La Plata

Guayama

Arecibo Observatory

Manatí

Río de Chuco

Barranquitas

Coamo

Río Grande de Manatí

Tibes Indigenous Heritage Center

Caribbean Sea

Arecibo

Lago Dos Bocas

Utuado

Cerro de Punta
(4,389 ft)

Ponce Museum of Art

Río Camuy Cave Park

Río Grande de Arecibo

Lares

Cordillera Central

Adjuntas

Ponce

Isabela

Camuy

Lago de Guajataca

San Sebastián

Río Culebrina

Yauco

Río Yauco

Aguadilla

Añasco

Mayagüez

San Germán

Guánica Forest Reserve

Aguada

Río Grande de Añasco

Porta Coeli

Boqueron

Cabo Rojo Lighthouse

plenty of bustling shops and restaurants, a stroll at twilight down the quiet side streets is magical.

Of course, Old San Juan is just a tiny corner of a modern, bustling metropolis. The Río Piedras area houses the University of Puerto Rico, where buildings are often festooned with political slogans, and the Río Piedras Market, where rows of stalls sell fruits, vegetables, and clothes. There are dozens of hotels right on the beach in San Juan, but to see the island in all its splendor, you'll want to get out of town.

HEAD FOR THE HILLS

Though sun and sand may represent Puerto Rico in travel posters, the island's mountains are just as spectacular. The bigger cities, and of course the beaches, are arranged in a ring around the coast. Leaving this loop to go inland inevitably means going up, up, up. Narrow, winding roads zigzag up the hillsides. You'll often gasp as cars hurtle toward you around tight curves. Roadside stands selling fruit and barbecued meat dot a scenic road called the Ruta Panoramica. Around every turn, some lucky family has a house nestled in the hills with a dazzling view.

The mountains of the Cordillera Central are incredibly lush. In some places, the hills seem to foam with vegetation. And if you ascend to the top of any peak, you can usually find a town—and a traffic jam. One of the most beautiful mountain towns is San Germán, which is famous for an austere chapel named Porta Coeli, or "the Gates of Heaven," which dates from 1606. The church's ceiling still contains the original beams, made of nearly indestructible

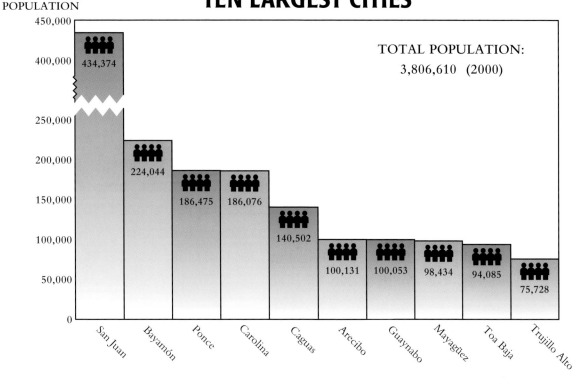

TEN LARGEST CITIES

POPULATION

TOTAL POPULATION:
3,806,610 (2000)

City	Population
San Juan	434,374
Bayamón	224,044
Ponce	186,475
Carolina	186,076
Caguas	140,502
Arecibo	100,131
Guaynabo	100,053
Mayagüez	98,434
Toa Baja	94,085
Trujillo Alto	75,728

ausubo wood. The second-oldest Spanish settlement in Puerto Rico, San Germán boasts gorgeous central plazas and startling views from the houses hugging the steep hillsides.

Another historic mountain town is Lares, site of the 1868 uprising known as El Grito de Lares. You can read about the proud history of the independence movement on the walls of the local ice cream parlor, Heladería Lares, which opened in 1968, on the one hundredth anniversary of the uprising. The store's offerings include an array of ice cream flavors based on local foods like avocado, corn, beans, rice, tomatoes, carrots, celery, sugarcane, ginger, and green beans. Be daring—you can taste before you buy.

KARST AND CAVES

The northwest part of the island is karst country, filled with lumpy, improbable shapes created when limestone caves collapse to create pits called sinkholes. Scientists took advantage of one of these deep circular pits to build a giant radio-antenna dish for the Arecibo Observatory. This vast bowl, a thousand feet wide and lined with 40,000 aluminum mirrors, focuses radio waves from outer space onto a platform suspended 450 feet in the air. It is the largest radio telescope in the world, and its location near the equator lets it scan the skies of both the northern and southern hemispheres, listening for signals from the far reaches of the universe. Scientists at Arecibo have made some amazing discoveries, including finding the first planets outside our solar system.

The telescope is also used to listen for signs of intelligent life. The observatory was featured in the movie *Contact*, in which Jodie Foster played a scientist who received messages from aliens. Even if you're not interested in science, you'll like the drive through the karst country that surrounds the telescope. It's almost like being on another planet in its own right.

Not too far from the observatory is the Río Camuy Cave Park. The underground rivers that dissolved the limestone to make sinkholes and karst also carved miles of underground caves. In 1958, an amazing cave network was discovered near Camuy. Tour guides lead visitors through an awe-inspiring underground chamber 200

The giant radio antenna at the Arecibo Observatory fills a natural sinkhole in the midst of odd-shaped hills called karst.

feet wide and 170 feet high. You can peer 150 feet down at the ancient river that began carving the cave 45 million years ago. Rippled ribbons of rock called draperies decorate the walls, and hanging formations called stalactites cling to the ceilings. Formed by minerals left by the dripping water, these stone icicles take a thousand years to grow one inch. So many bats live in Río Camuy

Cave that when the people making the movie *Batman Forever* needed bat sounds for their soundtrack, they came to these echoing caverns to record them.

BACK TO THE BEACH

If you descend the mountains to the western coast, you'll find some of Puerto Rico's most interesting beaches. In the northwest corner, steep red cliffs drop right to the water. You'll also find some beaches with high winds and waves, making them popular with surfers.

At the southwest corner is the popular swimming beach of Boquerón. Rows of palm trees, neatly mowed grass, and a vast expanse of white sand make it a leisurely place for sunning and swimming. You won't find plants, coral, or fish at Boquerón, just the calm water and soft sand that Puerto Ricans consider the perfect beach.

Barely twenty miles away, at the island's southwest corner, are Puerto Rico's steepest cliffs. At the Cabo Rojo Lighthouse, you can walk out on a narrow ridge that drops straight down on both sides for hundreds of feet. If you're not scared, your parents will be. At this windswept point, you feel like you are at the end of the world. The bumpy dirt road leading to the lighthouse is nearly impassable after a rain, but the slow trip is made enchanting by the many crabs that scuttle along the road, holding their claws in the air.

The lovely town of Aguada, on the northwest coast, is one of Puerto Rico's oldest settlements. It is near the site of Columbus's first landing.

The southwest is the island's dry side. At the Guánica Forest Reserve, you can see the strange sight of cactuses growing right next to the beach. It's the wildest, most exotic place on the island. Where a dirt road ends, you can walk into the reserve along the

At the Cabo Rojo Lighthouse, thin cliffs jut into the sea. "It's like a bridge to nothing. It's scary," said one visitor. "When the wind picks up, it feels like you're going to blow away."

rocky shore, feeling the bubbles of volcanic rock crunch beneath your feet. You won't find the smooth, white sand of the more popular beaches here, but you can wade into the water and see plants, rocks, and countless tropical fish in a variety of stripes and colors.

It's like climbing into an aquarium. Just across the road, the harsh landscape is filled with flowering cactuses and spiny, poisonous plants. Farther inland, trails lead through a forest that houses more species of birds than any other place on the island. Walk a few hundred feet and you'll see flashes of red and green and hear chirping sounds on all sides.

In the middle of the southern coast is the city of Ponce, known as *La Perla del Sur*, or "the Pearl of the South." Though Ponce is Puerto Rico's second-largest city, it feels very different from modern, urban San Juan. Founded in 1692, Ponce is centered on a lovely square filled with trees and fountains. Surrounding the square is a historic district of handsome buildings. The town hall is open and welcoming, with airy courtyards and hallways lined with paintings by leading Puerto Rican artists. Right on the square is perhaps the brightest building in Puerto Rico, the red-and-black striped Parque de Bombas, a former fire station. Decorated with curlicues and firefighting memorabilia, it looks more like a children's playhouse or a stage set than a real, grown-up building. You should also stop by the grand, spacious Ponce Museum of Art, which is filled with paintings by European masters and Puerto Rico's finest artists, including José Campeche and Francisco Oller y Cestero.

A must for anyone interested in the island's Native American history is the Tibes Indigenous Heritage Center just outside of Ponce. This site was discovered in 1975, when Hurricane Eloise flooded the city. When the waters receded, ancient artifacts were exposed. Tibes was the island's largest ceremonial meeting place for the Taínos and their ancestors. Ten ball courts, or *bateyes*, have been reconstructed, the biggest 111 by 118 feet. You can also walk inside

Ponce's brightest building, the Parque de Bombas, was used as a firehouse for more than a hundred years, from 1885 to 1990.

some reconstructed houses. A small but excellent museum contains pottery and carved stone sculptures made by the island's early inhabitants. It also has displays about their food, clothing, and customs, such as inhaling a drug they believed let them talk with spirits and see the future. One visitor recognized the gourds the Indians used for bowls, which looked just like the one his grandfather had—he refused to eat from anything else.

PONCE ON THE MARCH

The beauty of downtown Ponce stands as a shining example of what can be done with a little government spending. In the 1980s, the grand buildings of Ponce's historic zone were in ruins. Then a man from Ponce, Rafael Hernández Colón, became governor and shifted $600 million of government money to his neglected hometown. Under a program called Ponce on the March, hundreds of stately buildings were restored, wires were hidden from view, and the city reclaimed its title as Pearl of the South. The funding was yanked when a new governor was elected. If you stroll through Ponce today, you can clearly see the boundary of the restored area. On one side, pastel-painted mansions and hotels stand in all their former glory. On the other, crumbling walls give a hint of the grandeur that once was, and may one day be again when the political winds shift.

Heading back toward San Juan, stop in Coamo, Puerto Rico's third-oldest town. Coamo is in a valley, encircled by lumpy hills that makes it feel like it is in a world of its own. Near Coamo are hot springs that residents have been enjoying for hundreds, if not thousands, of years. The hot springs now flow into two huge swimming pools that can accomodate entire families of health-seekers.

On the eastern tip of the island, you can catch a ferry to Vieques. It's a beautiful ride, and you pass by several smaller islands on the way. After the crowds and traffic of the big island, when you reach Vieques you finally feel like you've gotten away to a real tropical paradise. Even the tourist town of Esperanza is just a small cluster of buildings. You can snorkel right under the town pier and see lots of fish, or swim ten minutes out to a smaller island surrounded by plants, fish, and coral. Esperanza is about the only town in Puerto Rico without a traffic jam. But on Saturday nights there is a people jam when everyone comes out to stroll back and forth on the main street by the beach.

If Vieques isn't quiet enough for you, try the even wilder island of Culebra. Much of it has been set aside as a wildlife refuge. It's as close to pure nature as you'll get, with great beaches and snorkeling.

A WALK IN THE RAIN FOREST

If you have time for only one side trip from San Juan, the place to visit is El Yunque rain forest. One of the most beautiful sights in Puerto Rico, it is less than an hour's drive from the city. It's amazing to think you can go so quickly from nerve-jangling, car-choked urban sprawl to an actual tropical rain forest. Because the Luquillo

TINY SHOOTING STARS

The most magical place in Puerto Rico is Mosquito Bay on the island of Vieques. The water here actually glows in the dark. It is filled with billions of tiny creatures called dinoflagellates that produce a burst of light when jostled. If your boat startles a fish, you'll see streaks of light in the water as it darts away. If you jump in for a swim, each movement will leave a glowing trail. Cup the water in your hand and it sparkles like fairy dust. "People often tell me this is the most incredible thing they've ever seen," says one tour guide.

Mosquito Bay connects to the ocean by a single narrow channel. This keeps the glowing creatures penned in like fireflies in a bottle. Each gallon of water in Mosquito Bay contains 720,000 dinoflagellates. There were once many more places like this in the world, but only a handful are left. Some were destroyed by widening the channel, causing the dinoflagellates to flow out to sea. Others were destroyed by pollution. A similar bay near La Parguera on the main island was once as dazzling as Mosquito Bay. Because of pollution, it is now only a tenth as bright as it once was.

To keep Mosquito Bay alive, tour guides don't use polluting gas powerboats. But you can see the bay from a quiet electric boat, or by paddling out in a kayak. Come here before the moon rises, and you simply won't believe your eyes.

Mountains catch the clouds sweeping in from the northeast, it rains there nearly every day. El Yunque gets 100 billion gallons of rain a year.

This is the greenest place on a very green island. It's so wet that some plants have "drip tip" leaves, with little spouts that channel off water so they won't rot or grow fungus. Plants grow on top of plants—orchids grow on tree trunks, with vines draped over the lot. It feels like a fairy-tale jungle filled with the songs of coquís.

The biggest pleasure at El Yunque is watching the clouds float in. No matter how sunny it is, it won't take long before you'll see a cloud floating toward the mountain. If you're near the top, it will be coming straight toward you. Tendrils of mist collect against the hillside and suddenly you're enveloped in fog. The fog thickens until you can't see a thing. Then comes the rain. In five minutes you're drenched—even your shoes are filled with water. At times like this, you can stumble along a trail to a scenic lookout point, and there's nothing to look at—you can't see ten feet. But if you wait long enough the clouds pass, and the valley slowly clears. You can look across an expanse of mist at another peak that minutes ago was invisible. Then the clouds move on, and you can see the whole valley and the sea in the distance. It's magnificent.

THE FLAG: *The Puerto Rico flag consists of three red and two white stripes, with a dark blue triangle against the side. Inside the triangle is a white five-pointed star. The flag was adopted in 1952.*

THE SEAL: *A lamb in the center of the Puerto Rico seal symbolizes peace. Above the lamb are the letters F and I, which stand for Ferdinand and Isabella, the Spanish king and queen when Columbus arrived at Puerto Rico.*

COMMONWEALTH SURVEY

Status: Puerto Rico became a commonwealth July 25, 1952

Origin of Name: *Puerto Rico* is Spanish for "rich port."

Nickname: Isle of Enchantment

Capital: San Juan

Motto: John Is His Name

Bird: Stripe-headed tanager (*reinita mora*)

Animal: Coquí

Flower: Puerto Rican hibiscus (*flor de maga*)

Tree: Silk-cotton tree (*ceiba*)

Stripe-headed tanager

Puerto Rican hibiscus

LA BORINQUEÑA

Borinquen was the original name of the island that the Spaniards renamed Puerto Rico. The song "La Borinqueña" is widely recognized as the anthem of Puerto Rico.

La_____ tier - ra de ¡Bo - rin - quen! Don - de he na - ci - do
Oh,_____ my land of Bo - rin - quen! The land where I was

yo,_____ Es_____ un jar - dín flo - ri - do,
born,_____ Gar - den so full of flow - ers,

de má - gi - co pri - mor'. Un cie - lo siem - pre ní - ti - do,
ma - gic - 'ly won - der - ful. Her sky for - ev - er lu - mi - nous,

la sir - ve de do - sel, Y dan ar - ru - llos plá - ci - dos
is like a can - o - py, And the waves gen - tle lull - a - by

las o - las a sus pies. ¸Cuan - do a sus pla - ya lle - gó Co -
is a soft mel - o - dy. And when to this land Co - lum - bus

GEOGRAPHY

Highest Point: 4,389 feet above sea level, at Cerro de Punta

Lowest Point: Sea level, on the coast

Area: 3,515 square miles including Culebra, Mona, and Vieques islands

Greatest Distance, North to South: 39 miles

Greatest Distance, East to West: 111 miles

Hottest Recorded Temperature: 103° F at San Lorenzo on August 22, 1906

Coldest Recorded Temperature: 40° F at Aibonito on March 9, 1911

Average Annual Precipitation: 70 inches in the north, 37 inches in the south

Major Rivers: Añasco, Arecibo, Bayamón, Culebrinas, La Plata, Loíza, Yauco

Major Lakes: Caonillas, Cartagena, Cidra, Guajataca, Loíza, San José

Trees: African tulip, ausubo, bay cedar, breadfruit, ceiba, coconut palm, flamboyan, mahogany, mangrove, tabonuco, yagrumo hembra

Wild Plants: bunch grass, cactus, damiana, guitarán, hibiscus, orchid, poinsettia, rubber vine, tree fern

Ceiba

Animals: anole, bat, coquí, cucubano, iguana, manatee, mongoose, snake

Iguana

Birds: gorrion, heron, hummingbird, nightingale, oriole, owl, Puerto Rican bullfinch, thrasher

Fish: angelfish, barracuda, herring, marlin, mullet, pompano, shark, snapper, Spanish mackerel, tuna

Endangered Animals: brown pelican, Caribbean monk seal, Culebra Island giant anole, finback whale, hawksbill sea turtle, leatherback sea turtle, Monito gecko, Puerto Rican boa, Puerto Rican broad-winged hawk, Puerto Rican nightjar, Puerto Rican parrot, Puerto Rican plain pigeon, Puerto Rican sharp-shinned hawk, sperm whale, Virgin Islands tree boa, West Indian manatee, yellow-shouldered blackbird

Puerto Rican parrot

Endangered Plants: *Adiantum vivesii*, *Aristida chaseae*, *Auerodendron pauciflorum*, bariaco, beautiful goetzea, *Calyptranthes thomasiana*, capa rosa, *Catesbaea melanocarpa*, *Chamaecrista glandulosa mirabilis*, chupacallos, Cook's holly, *Cordia bellonis*, *Cranichis ricartii*, *Daphnopsis hellerana*, *Elaphoglossum serpens*, elfin tree fern, erubia, *Eugenia woodburyana*, higuero de sierra, *Ilex sintenisii*, *Lepanthes eltoroensis*, *Leptocereus grantianus*, *Lyonia truncata proctorii*, *Mitracarpus maxwelliae*, *Mitracarpus polycladus*, *Myrcia paganii*, palo colorado, palo de jazmin, palo de nigua, palo de ramon, palo de rosa, pelos del diablo, *Polystichum calderonense*, St. Thomas prickly-ash, *Tectaria estremerana*, *Ternstroemia subsessilis*, *Thelypteris inabonensis*, *Thelypteris verecunda*, *Thelypteris yaucoensis*, uvillo, Vahl's boxwood, *Vernonia proctorii*, West Indian walnut, Wheeler's peperonia

TIMELINE

Puerto Rico History

c. 2000 B.C. Indians begin living in Puerto Rico

c. 400 B.C. Ancestors of the Taínos come to Puerto Rico from South America

1400s Taíno Indians live in small villages around the island, raising crops and fishing

1493 Italian explorer Christopher Columbus lands in Puerto Rico on his second voyage to the Americas

1508 Spaniard Juan Ponce de León founds Caparra, the first European settlement on the island

1511 The Taínos rebel against the Spaniards and are defeated; a few survivors retreat to the mountains

1518 The first African slaves are brought to Puerto Rico

1539 Spanish colonists start building El Morro fortress

1598 The English seize San Juan and hold it for five months

1625 Dutch sailors attack and burn San Juan

1812 The constitution of 1812 gives Puerto Ricans basic civil rights

1855 An outbreak of the disease cholera kills 30,000 Puerto Ricans

1868 In the so-called El Grito de Lares uprising, revolutionary leader Ramón Emeterio Betances declares an independent Republic of Puerto Rico. The rebellion is soon crushed.

1898 The United States wins the Spanish-American War and takes control of Puerto Rico

1917 The Jones Act makes Puerto Ricans U.S. citizens

1928 A hurricane devastates Puerto Rico's coffee and sugarcane plantations

1932 Puerto Rican women win the right to vote

1937 Nineteen people are killed in the Ponce Massacre, as police put a stop to a nationalist demonstration in Ponce

1949 Luis Muñoz Marín becomes Puerto Rico's first elected governor

1952 Puerto Rico becomes a commonwealth

1985 Heavy rains and flooding on the island cause 200 deaths

1998 Hurricane Georges strikes Puerto Rico, causing $2 billion in damage

2000 Puerto Ricans elect their first woman governor, Sila M. Calderón

ECONOMY

Agricultural Products: bananas, beef, coffee, milk, pineapples, sugar, tobacco

Tobacco

Manufactured Products: clothing, food products, electrical equipment, machinery, medicine, rum, scientific instruments

Natural Resources: clay, copper, lime, nickel, sand and gravel

Business and Trade: finance, health care, real estate, tourism, wholesale and retail trade

CALENDAR OF CELEBRATIONS

Coffee Harvest Festival At this February event in Maricao, you can look out over beautiful coffee plantations, see how coffee beans are roasted, and watch traditional *café con leche* (coffee with milk) being made.

Carnaval One of Puerto Rico's wildest parties happens around February in Ponce. For six days just before Lent, the Christian time of fasting before Easter, musicians and dancers parade through the streets wearing colorful costumes and masks.

Dulce Sueño Paso Fino Horse Show Puerto Rico races its special breed of Paso Fino horses in Guayama each March. *Paso fino* means "fine step," and the breed is known for giving an incredibly smooth ride.

Sugar Festival In April, San Germán throws a feast in honor of sugarcane, one of the island's most important crops. Check out the cane farming exhibitions and enjoy some local foods.

Danza Festival This weeklong festival in Ponce celebrates the *danza*, Puerto Rico's elegant ballroom dance. Beautifully dressed couples turn and sway to orchestra music on Plaza las Delicias.

Casals Festival Famous musicians from around the world come to San Juan to perform at this June festival, founded by renowned cellist Pablo Casals.

San Juan Bautista Day On June 21, San Juan throws a huge celebration for its patron saint, known in English as St. John the Baptist. You can join the colorful processions in town, or honor the saint the traditional way, by walking backward three times into the sea.

Aibonito Flower Festival Brilliant roses, carnations, lilies, and begonias fill the little mountain town of Aibonito in June. Visitors love to stroll past the flowers and breathe in their sweet perfume.

Fiesta de Santiago Apostol Puerto Rico shows off its African roots at the end of July in Loíza. Groups of drummers keep the beat as people in amazing costumes dance for Santiago (St. James), Loíza's patron saint.

Jayuya Indigenous Festival In mid-November, Jayuya celebrates the culture of Puerto Rico's early settlers. Visitors can enjoy traditional Taíno games, food, and music.

Bomba y Plena Festival Drummers, dancers, and singers gather in Ponce each November, filling the air with Puerto Rico's African-inspired *bomba* and *plena* music.

Hatillo Masks Festival On December 28, masked devils stalk the streets of Hatillo, pretending to be agents of King Herod, who ordered that all male infants be killed after Jesus was born.

COMMONWEALTH STARS

Julia de Burgos (1914–1953) was one of Puerto Rico's best-known poets. Like the Chilean poet Pablo Neruda who inspired her, she wrote about personal experiences, such as loneliness and love, as well as political ones, like the need for freedom. In her most famous poem, "Río Grande de Loíza," she shows how the life of a person and a river intertwine. Burgos was born in Carolina.

José Campeche (1752–1809), Puerto Rico's first great painter, was also a talented musician, sculptor, and architect. His mother was a Spaniard from the Canary Islands, and his father, a former slave, was a master woodcarver. Campeche was born in San Juan. After studying painting there, Campeche produced close to 400 portraits, religious pictures, and historical scenes, becoming one of Latin America's most respected artists. Campeche's paintings can be seen in many Puerto Rican churches.

Pablo Casals (1876–1973) was a celebrated cellist and conductor. Casals's musical talent blossomed when he was a young boy growing up in Spain. By the 1930s, he was known the world over for showing his expressive cello music. In 1956, Casals moved to Puerto Rico, where his mother had been born. For the rest of his life, he shared his passion for music with other people on the island. His presence is still felt during the Casals Festival in San Juan.

Pablo Casals

Roberto Clemente (1934–1972) was one of the best outfielders baseball has ever known. Clemente, who was born in Carolina, played with the Pittsburgh Pirates for 17 years. His powerful throwing arm won him 12 Golden Glove awards, and in 1966 he was named the National League's Most Valuable Player. Fans were crushed when Clemente died in a plane crash while trying to deliver supplies to the victims of an earthquake. He was inducted into the Baseball Hall of Fame in 1973.

Angel Cordero Jr. (1942–   ), a native of San Juan, is a champion jockey known for his competitive drive. Cordero's father and grandfather were also jockeys, and he started riding at age 17. A few years later he moved to New York, where he earned a reputation as a talented racer who could get his horses to give their all. By the time he retired at age 50, Cordero had won more than 7,000 races, including three Kentucky Derbies, the most famous horse race in the United States.

Angel Cordero Jr.

José de Diego (1866–1921) was a brilliant poet and a founder of Puerto Rico's independence movement. A native of Aguadilla, Diego became active in politics as a young man. He helped start the Autonomist and Unionist political parties, both dedicated to giving Puerto Rico control over its own destiny. A talented speaker, journalist, and essay writer, he made a lasting mark on the literary world with his beautiful romantic poems.

José Feliciano (1945–   ) is a world-renowned singer and guitarist. Feliciano was born in Lares and moved to New York City with his family when he was five. Blind from birth, he taught himself music by listening to records. He first learned to play a small accordian and later the guitar. Over the years, Feliciano's soft voice and masterful guitar style have won him countless fans and six Grammy Awards. "Light My Fire" and "Feliz Navidad" are among his best-known songs.

José Feliciano

Rosario Ferré (1938–   ) is a writer whose stories and novels struggle with important Puerto Rican social issues. Ferré was born in Ponce and studied literature at the University of Puerto Rico. She founded and edited a magazine in the 1970s, and later wrote for the newspapers *El Nuevo Día* and the *San Juan Star*. Ferré's first novel, *Maldito Amor*, was published in 1988. Her other books include *La Casa de la Laguna* and *Vecindarios Excentricos*.

Rafael Hernández (1892–1965) composed of some of Puerto Rico's best-loved popular songs. Hernández was born in Aguadilla and had a successful music career in both Puerto Rico and the United States. To many Puerto Ricans, his ballads "Lamento Borincano," "Capullito de Alelí," and "Preciosa" are as much a symbol of the island as sandy beaches and palm trees.

Eugenio María de Hostos y Bonilla (1839–1903) was a leading teacher and social reformer. Born in Mayagüez, Hostos was an early supporter of Puerto Rican independence. He was educated in Spain, became a professor at the University of Chile, and helped reform the education system in the Dominican Republic. The author of many respected essays, Hostos became famous throughout Latin America, both for his political views and his graceful ability to express them.

Raul Julia (1940–1994) was a successful stage and screen actor. A native of San Juan, Julia fell in love with acting while playing the devil in a school play. In 1964, he gave his first New York performance, appearing in the Spanish production *La Vida es un Sueño* (Life Is a Dream). A natural performer, he later acted in everything from Shakespeare to musicals. Julia also starred in a wide range of movies, including *Kiss of the Spider Woman* and *The Addams Family*.

Raul Julia

Hector Lavoe (1946–1993) was the greatest salsa singer of the 1960s and 1970s. Born Hector Juan Perez in Ponce, he hit New York's Latin music scene at age 17. Taking the stage name Lavoe (Spanish slang for "the voice"), he teamed up with trombonist Willie Colon and then sang with his own band. He attracted fans as much with his warm personality as with his amazing singing style. "Mi Gente" and "De Ti Depende" are two of his most popular songs.

Luis Llorens Torres (1878–1945) wrote beautiful poetry about what it means to be Puerto Rican. Llorens Torres was born in Juana Díaz, was educated in Spain, and later worked as a lawyer. In 1913, he helped found a literary magazine that took Puerto Rican poetry in a new direction. Llorens Torres was known as a *criollo* poet, which means he believed it was important to develop a special Puerto Rican style. One of his most celebrated poems is "Canción de las Antillas" (Song of the Antilles).

Ricky Martin (1971–   ) is the world's most popular Latin music star. Martin's good looks and great voice gave him a head start in the show business world. Born in San Juan, he started doing television commercials at age 6 and joined the teen singing group Menudo when he was 12. In 1998, Martin shot to stardom with his hit single "La Copa de la Vida" from the album *Vuelve*, which brought him a Grammy Award. His hard-driving blend of rock, pop, and salsa has made him the best-selling Latin artist of all time.

Ricky Martin

Rita Moreno (1931–   ) is an actress who has helped expand the role of Hispanic women in show business. Born in Humacao, Moreno moved to New York when she was very young. She was dancing on Broadway by the age of 13. During her acting career, Moreno often had to play the part of the hot-tempered Latina, but her talent went far beyond that role. In 1962, she won an Academy Award for her performance in *West Side Story*. She later acted in children's television, earning an Emmy Award for her work on *The Muppet Show*.

Luis Muñoz Marín (1898–1980), Puerto Rico's first elected governor, was an outstanding leader and champion of the poor. The founder of the island's Popular Democratic Party, he worked to improve the lives of ordinary Puerto Ricans. Muñoz Marín served as governor from 1949 to 1965, was an author of Puerto Rico's constitution, and helped the island become a commonwealth in 1952. Muñoz Marín was born in San Juan and educated in Washington, D.C.

Luis Muñoz Marín

Juan "Chi Chi" Rodríguez (1935–   ) is a professional golfer known for his flamboyant style. Rodríguez was born in Río Piedras, where his father made a hard living cutting sugarcane. As a young boy, he used to practice his swing on tin cans instead of golf balls, using a club he made from the branch of a guava tree. Rodríguez rose to the top of professional golf in the 1960s. In 1979, he used part of his earnings to set up a foundation for troubled teens.

Juan "Chi Chi" Rodríguez

Tito Rodríguez (1923–1973) is a legend of the New York Latin music scene. Born in San Juan, Rodríguez moved to the United States in 1939 to sing in his brother's band. He rose to fame in the 1940s and 1950s, when mambo, a big band style of Latin jazz, became popular. He led his own band starting in 1947, and for years he battled drummer Tito Puente for the title of Mambo King.

Luis Rafael Sanchez (1936–   ) is one of Puerto Rico's most respected writers. Sanchez was born in Humacao and studied theater at the University of Puerto Rico. His plays and novels are known for their rhythmic language, mixing everyday speech with older Spanish words. Sanchez writes most often about what it's like to be Puerto Rican. His novel *La*

Guaracha del Macho Camacho (Macho Comacho's Beat), a comedy set in San Juan, brought him international acclaim.

Gilberto Santa Rosa (1962–   ), a native of San Juan, is known as the Gentleman of Salsa. Santa Rosa began studying music when he was 12, and sang with others before forming his own band. Santa Rosa is famous for improvising instead of singing his music the same way each time. In 1995, Santa Rosa became the first Puerto Rican salsa singer to perform at New York's Carnegie Hall.

Felix Trinidad (1973–   ) is a boxer whose powerful punch is respected around the world. In 1993, he defeated two-time world champion Maurice Blocker to take the International Boxing Federation welterweight crown. By 2001, he had slugged his way to the World Boxing Association welterweight, super welterweight and middleweight titles, and was still undefeated. Trinidad lives in Cupey Alto.

TOUR THE ISLAND

Old San Juan Hundreds of pastel-colored buildings and shaded plazas make up the heart of the Puerto Rican capital.

El Morro (San Juan) It's great to watch the pounding surf from atop this 460-year-old fortress at the edge of San Juan Bay. You can also tour the secret tunnels behind its 20-foot-thick walls.

Río Camuy Cave Park (Lares) The Taíno Indians believed sacred spirits lived in this underground wonderland, one of the largest cave networks in the world. A highlight is 170-foot-high Clara Cave.

Mona Island Just 45 miles from the main island of Puerto Rico, this island is full of wildlife, including sea turtles, iguanas, and more than 100 species of birds.

Porta Coeli Church (San Germán) Built in 1606, this is the oldest church in the United States. The enormous doors are made of wood from the Puerto Rican ausubo tree.

El Yunque (Palmer) The Caribbean National Forest takes its nickname from the good Taíno spirit *Yukiyú*. Millions of tiny tree frogs are hidden among its ferns and palms.

El Yunque

Ponce Museum of Art (Ponce) Paintings from Spain, Italy, Holland, France, Britain, and Puerto Rico are on display at this art museum.

Las Cabezas de San Juan Nature Preserve (Fajardo) A guided tour of this protected stretch of coast will take you past coral reefs, mangrove forests, and quiet lagoons. A lighthouse stands on a 200-foot cliff above the sea.

San Juan Cathedral (San Juan) This ancient church contains explorer Juan Ponce de León's tomb.

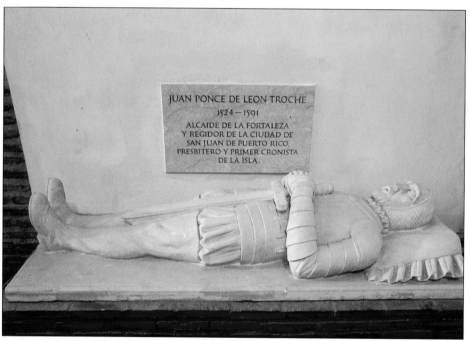

San Juan Cathedral

Toro Negro Forest Reserve This forest surrounds Cerro de Punta, Puerto Rico's highest peak. The lush, rugged landscape is threaded with waterfalls.

Luquillo Beach (Luquillo) One of the island's most beautiful beaches lies in a crescent-shaped bay edged by a coconut grove.

Tropical Agriculture Research Station (Mayagüez) In these vast gardens you can see how local crops like cacao, spices, yams, and bananas are grown.

Capilla del Cristo (San Juan) Statues of saints crowd this outdoor chapel next to the Parque de las Palomas. The silver ornaments they wear stand for healing miracles the saints are said to have performed.

Guánica Forest Reserve (Guánica) This landscape on the dry side of Puerto Rico features many kinds of cactus and some of the island's most colorful birds.

Mosquito Bay (Vieques) When you pass through the waters of this bay at night you leave a bright trail of light, cast by tiny underwater creatures that glow like fireflies.

Caguana Indian Ceremonial Park (Caguana) This shady park marks the ancient courts where Taíno Indians once played their ball game *batey*. Some of the rocks that surround the courts are covered with Taíno drawings.

Museum of Puerto Rican Music (Ponce) Puerto Rican musical instruments of all kinds are on display here, including local favorites like the güiro and the maracas.

Hacienda Buena Vista (Ponce) This mountainside farm was once a rich producer of coffee. The house and mill are preserved as they were in the 1800s, when crops were collected in giant bowls made from the root of the ceiba tree.

FUN FACTS

The flavoring ingredients for Coca-Cola and Pepsi are made in the town of Cidra.

Many words we use today are descended from the Taíno language, including hurricane, hammock, and canoe.

The deepest waters of the Atlantic Ocean are located just off of Puerto Rico. About 75 miles north of the island is a depression of the sea floor called the Puerto Rico Trench. One end plunges into the Milwaukee Depth, where the ocean is more than five miles deep.

FIND OUT MORE

Would you like to learn more about Puerto Rico? You could start by checking your local library or bookstore for these titles:

GENERAL BOOKS

Davis, Lucille. *Puerto Rico*. New York: Children's Press, 2000.

Thompson, Kathleen. *Puerto Rico*. Austin, TX: Raintree/Steck-Vaughn, 1995.

SPECIAL INTEREST BOOKS

Bernier-Grand, Carmen. *Poet and Politician of Puerto Rico: Don Luis Muñoz Marín*. New York: Orchard, 1995.

Mike, Jan. *Juan Bobo and the Horse of Seven Colors: A Puerto Rican Legend*. New York: Troll, 1995. One of many traditional humorous stories about Juan Bobo, or Foolish John, a popular character in Puerto Rican folklore.

Silva Lee, Alfonso. *Coquí y Sus Amigos / Coquí and His Friends*. St. Paul, MN: Pangaea, 2000. An introduction to the wildlife of Puerto Rico, with dazzling color photos and text in both English and Spanish.

Walker, Paul Robert. *Pride of Puerto Rico: The Life of Roberto Clemente*. New York: Harcourt Brace, 1998.

FICTION

Bernier-Grand, Carmen. *In the Shade of the Nispero Tree*. New York: Orchard, 1999. Class and skin color come between two fourth-grade friends.

Mohr, Nicholosa. *Felita*. New York: Puffin, 1999. Eight-year-old Felita moves to a new neighborhood, where she is teased because she is from Puerto Rico.

Mohr, Nicholosa. *Going Home*. New York: Puffin, 1999. Twelve-year-old Felita, frustrated by her strict family in New York, spends the summer with her uncle in Puerto Rico.

FOR OLDER READERS

López, Alfredo. *Doña Licha's Island: Modern Colonialism in Puerto Rico*. Boston: South End, 1987. A discussion of how Puerto Rico has suffered from colonialism, by a journalist who favors Puerto Rican independence.

Santiago, Roberto, ed. *Boricuas: Influential Puerto Rican Writers—An Anthology*. New York: One World/Ballantine, 1995. Dozens of Puerto Rican writers explore what it means to be Puerto Rican, on and off the island.

Santiago, Esmerelda. *When I Was Puerto Rican*. New York: Vintage, 1994. Memories of growing up in Puerto Rico.

MUSIC

Putumayo Presents: Puerto Rico. Putumayo, 2000. A collection of the many styles of Puerto Rican music.

Puente, Tito. *50 Years of Swing: 50 Great Years & Tracks*. Uni/RMM, 1997. A 3-CD box set from Tito Puente.

INTERNET

http://welcome.topuertorico.org
Filled with information about the people, places, and culture of Puerto Rico.

INDEX

Page numbers for charts, graphs, and illustrations are in boldface.